WHEN SOMEONE ASKS FOR HELP

A Practical
Guide
for Counseling

Everett L. Worthington, Jr.

InterVarsity Press
Downers Grove
Illinois 60515

© 1982 by Inter-Varsity Christian Fellowship of the United States of America

All rights reserved. No part of this book may be reproduced in any form without written permission from InterVarsity Press, Downers Grove, Illinois.

InterVarsity Press is the book-publishing division of Inter-Varsity Christian Fellowship, a student movement active on campus at hundreds of universities, colleges and schools of nursing. For information about local and regional activities, write IVCF, 233 Langdon St., Madison, WI 53703.

Distributed in Canada through InterVarsity Press, 1875 Leslie St., Unit 10, Don Mills, Ontario M3B 2M5, Canada.

Unless otherwise stated, quotations from the Bible are from the Revised Standard Version, copyrighted 1946, 1952, © 1971, 1973, by the Division of Christian Education, National Council of the Churches of Christ in the USA, and used by permission.

ISBN 0-87784-375-9

Printed in the United States of America

Library of Congress Cataloging in Publication Data

Worthington, Everett L., 1946-
　　When someone asks for help.

　　Includes bibliographical references.
　　1. Counseling.　I. Title.
BF637.C6W67　　　　　　253.5　　　　　　82-81
ISBN 0-87784-375-9　　　　　　　　　　　AACR2

17	16	15	14	13	12	11	10	9	8	7	6	5	4	3	2
95	94	93	92	91	90	89	88	87	86	85	84	83

To Kirby, my wife,
and
Pastor Tom Allport
who showed me how
Christians love
and thus helped me
to know
Jesus

Preface

God has chosen to use people to fulfill his purposes. What a glorious mystery! What an awesome responsibility!

Part of our responsibility is to love others by helping those who are in the midst of problems and who want our help. Research shows that people who do not have formal training in counseling can nevertheless be effective helpers when they learn fundamental helping skills. This book will help you to effectively help others by using principles that are consistent with God's written revelation. It is aimed at Christians gifted by the Holy Spirit to give aid (Rom 12:8), many of whom are not professional helpers.

This book is a practical manual. Part one develops a foundation for Christian helping, which is rooted in the evangelical Christian tradition. I believe that God truly exists in three persons—God the Father, Jesus the Son and the Holy Spirit. I believe that each person of the Godhead is at work in the world. I believe that we find out about this work through the Holy Spirit and through God's Word, the Bible. Listening to God means listening to both his specific and general communications. Based on this knowledge, I describe how problems develop and I describe a five-stage model of how to help others.

In part two you will learn helping skills for each stage. Examples demonstrate how to use these skills while helping friends, but this model is not a cookbook of what to do in any situation. I hope that counselors of various theoretical orientations will agree substantially with the model because it describes what happens in counseling. The model is a metatheory of counseling: it describes the general process of counseling but leaves to the helper the task of understanding the specific causes and cures of emotional problems. Although the model is consistent with Scripture, it could not be gleaned solely from Scripture. The Bible was not intended to be a counseling manual, though it is helpful to people with problems.

I believe that this book will help you become a better helper. If you use the model and practice the skills that I suggest, I believe that you will feel more confident as you help people. The ability to help people is a gift of God. My prayer for you is that God, through the Holy Spirit of Jesus, will magnify his gift to you. That will glorify God.

Acknowledgments

In a book about helping, it is a pleasure to acknowledge all those who have helped. Foremost my thanks go to Kirby, my wife. She helped me with many ideas in the book. But more than this, she has supported and encouraged me, taught me to love, demonstrated Christian living, shown Jesus' love and helped me immeasurably. God was abundantly gracious when he brought us together.

Many people read and commented on portions of the manuscript in various forms and therefore helped me shape it: Geoff Sutton, Sherry Linger, Linda Zelenka and Mike Worthington. My brother has especially encouraged me by being a model of a good writer. Clients and friends provided stimulation and case material for the book, though I have tried to protect their identities and thus cannot thank them individually. Workshop participants and Sunday-school class members labored under earlier versions of these ideas about helping, and to them I am grateful. Rena Canipe has shown her love by providing a place for me to work and to vacation, and a vision of a loving Christian woman in action. Finally, the people of Christ Presbyterian Chapel have supported me with prayer and with their presence through the composition of this book.

Elizabeth Martin did much more than type the manuscript in her usual highly professional fashion. She also talked to me, encouraged me and gave me confidence in my work. She is a joy and an inspiration. My parents also deserve special recognition. They raised three Christian children—what greater testimony can there be?

1

Me, a
Helper?

Do you have a minute?" Charles asked.

It was Friday afternoon, and I had just dropped by his house to borrow a tool to repair my window. Something was bothering Charles, so we went inside. He dropped into his reclining chair, but he did not recline—he slumped forward. "Well, I have cancer," he said quickly, almost defiantly. "I can't believe it. I never had any idea! I didn't feel anything—pain, I mean. But, well, this morning the doctor told me that I have cancer. I feel so helpless."

Charles paused, his head in his hands. What could I say? What could I do? I felt as if my mind had been injected with novocaine.

"Oh, Charles," I finally said. "That's a real blow, isn't it? Kinda like being kicked in the stomach."

"Oh, it is. . . . It really is," he moaned.

"It really makes you think about all those things that you've taken for granted all these years."

"It sure does . . . especially about Margret." He looked down. "What's going to happen to her? Oh, Lord, I just don't know what to do."

"You don't know what to do about Margret?" I asked.

"Yeah, we always said that we wanted to die together. In an accident or a plane crash or something. Now I know that I only have a little while to live. What's that going to do to her? It's too much to bear."

"You're really concerned," I said. "You really don't know how Margret will react. It sounds like you haven't told her yet."

"I couldn't. I know that's wrong, but I had to think about it before I could speak to her. She's at the store now. I just don't know how to break it to her. I even lied to her when I got home from the doctor's this morning. I told her everything was fine. What can I do?"

After our prayers and an hour of talk, I went home exhausted and uneasy. Later, as I thought about that afternoon, I wondered why I, a trained counselor, should feel so uncomfortable when talking with Charles in this crisis. I had talked to so many people in my office—but that was different. Or was it?

I decided there were some important differences between formal counseling by a professional and informal counseling between friends. But I saw how my training in counseling *had* helped me comfort Charles, even though I felt uncomfortable myself. I thought about how difficult it is for people who have no training to know what to do when they are asked for help. I knew some excellent natural helpers. How did they feel? I wondered if sometimes they felt almost abandoned. If so, what could I do to help them become better helpers?

Friends at church told me that they had often been asked for advice, help or informal counseling by their friends. They also said how uncomfortable they felt in many situations. At their suggestion, I taught an adult Sunday-school course entitled "Lay Counseling: What to Do When Someone Has a Problem." The course was well attended and considered helpful. I incorporated participants' comments into a workshop format; these workshops, in turn, showed me that a practical book about counseling might be useful—a book that would aid Christians in helping people whom the Lord brings their way.

Why Is Friend-to-Friend Counseling Effective?
Many psychologists agree that more trained nonprofessional counselors are needed. As early as 1968 Robert Carkhuff, after summarizing much research about peer helpers, concluded that people helped by peer counselors do "as well as or better than" people helped by professional counselors.[1] In a variety of groups, trained nonprofessional counselors were very effective. Since Carkhuff's review, other researchers have also found that properly trained nonprofessional counselors can help people who have psychological problems.[2]

Recently several Christian psychologists have written books that teach Christians how to help other people within the church. For example, Gary Collins in *How to Be a People Helper* says that the purpose of counseling is to help people become disciples of Christ.[3] The major part of the book gives excellent general guidelines for crisis, suicide and telephone counseling, but lacks concrete advice on how to help a friend. In 1977 Lawrence Crabb wrote *Effective Biblical Counseling*, an excellent book aimed at professional Christian counselors and pastors who counsel often.[4] In one chapter Crabb applies his model of counseling to nonprofessionals, identifying three levels of counseling within the church. All Christians could listen to and encourage others. A few, such as elders or others specifically gifted for counseling, could be trained to use biblical approaches to solving problems. A select few, highly trained and gifted, could employ Crabb's full method. Paul Welter's book, *How to Help a Friend,* contains a three-step method for helping friends: determine the severity of the problem, the way people use what they have learned and the way people learn.[5] While Welter's approach is simple and practical, it tackles only a few of the problems that people typically encounter.

Two questions arise. Why are trained nonprofessionals often as effective as professionals, and what is unique about this book?

Professional and peer counseling are valuable at different times for different people. Professional counselors, as a group, are well trained and have experience helping people with a variety of personal problems. Their focus is primarily on the person as a client. The counselor has implicit permission to actively question the client and to ask the client to change his or her behavior. This can have good results. The client expects to reveal emotional secrets to the counselor; friends, however, do not always expect to reveal secrets to other friends. In addition, secrets may be shared with a professional without fear of hurting the friendship. The client believes the counselor will act professionally and, most importantly, will safeguard personal information. The client usually believes that the counselor can help. With peer counselors, a friend does not always believe he or she will receive help. Appointments will usually be scheduled once each week with a professional, yet friends do not generally meet together regularly. The counseling relationship, although often fostering strong attachment, will probably involve little personal contact other than appointments. On the negative side, professional counseling is often expensive (although sometimes community agencies use flexible fee scales so that most people can afford psychological help).

Friend-to-friend counseling is free, has no stigma attached to it and can be much less formal than professional counseling. Because most people have limited (or no) formal psychological training and limited counseling experience, the strength of lay counseling usually depends on the relationship between helper and friend. Personal (rather than professional) relationships can result in deep sharing but the focus is not always on the help seeker. When one friend is dealing with personal problems, the focus of the relationship is temporarily on that person, but in time a balance returns. The peer counselor has permission to ask about emotionally charged, personal details of a friend's life only to the (approximate) extent that he or she is willing to share important personal details with that friend. The depth of relationship between friends can be a great advantage.

Another advantage of friendship relationships over professional relationships is that a friend knows more about the help seeker's life and behavior than a professional counselor. The professional sees the client in only one situation, a formal interview, and knows only what the client talks about. Peer counselors, however, see their friends in many situations. They may know about the person's family, other friends, church, spiritual life, work, lifestyle and typical ways of handling problems. Thus, a friend is able to evaluate how much a problem is interfering with a person's life, how the problem is affecting the person's behavior, how well the person is coping with the problem and, perhaps, how clearly the person is seeing the problem.

In addition, the lay counselor is more like the help seeker than is the professional counselor. Friends are often of similar social class, education and background. Their language is similar, uncluttered by counseling jargon. They may have common interests and activities, which provide numerous sharing opportunities and room for give-and-take. Sometimes the friend is more available than the professional. Because rapport is already established, a friend is not concerned about starting a new relationship but can immediately begin to work with the friend on the specific problem.

It is little wonder that training nonprofessionals to use basic helping skills and providing them with a plan or model for helping people can often make them effective counselors. Many people need such help before deciding whether to approach a professional. In fact, the people who seek professional counseling are usually those who have not been sufficiently helped by their friends, families, pastor or church. These people are few, for most of the effective counseling is done by nonprofessionals. Many with emotional problems never need to see a professional because they are helped by friends.

What Can You Expect from This Book?

This book is practical. In it I describe a simple yet effective, five-step model for helping people solve problems. Then I cover the skills needed for each step of the model. Scattered throughout the book are examples of counseling dialogs, though I have changed names and details to protect the identity of friends and clients upon whose experience these dialogs are based. You will learn and see applied, step by step, a method of helping people, supplemented by exercises to improve your helping skills.

To find out what you have learned from reading this book, you need to compare what you know now with what you will know when you have finished the book. The best way to do that is to do some task now and later. Ideally, you could videotape a counseling session with a friend, then later compare your performance with the tape. For most people, however, that is not possible; consequently, at the beginning of my workshops on counseling I have each participant complete a case study on a fictitious person named Jim. I have included a description of Jim below. You should read about Jim and try to answer, in writing, the questions at the end of the description. Keep a copy of your answers. At the end of the book I have included another case study that you can use to measure your progress.

When I come to such exercises in books, I usually skip right over them without a backward glance. In this case, though, I encourage you to take the time to answer the questions about Jim. Workshop participants tell me that this is an invaluable, instructive exercise.

Jim: A Case Study

Jim, a twenty-six-year-old at your church, talked with you last week for about twenty-five minutes. Jim is discouraged. He is the only Christian in his office. All of his so-called friends give him a hard time about being a "Jesus freak." They say he is stupid to fall for that religious stuff. He has been under considerable pressure from his girlfriend, who is not a Christian, to stop attending church. He confesses that some sins that bothered him before he became a Christian have reappeared. These include anger, bitterness, bad language and gossip. He also mentions a "sexual sin" but seems too embarrassed to talk about it. Jim complains of often being nervous and scared. He also has a poor appetite and wakes up early, unable to get back to sleep because his "mind is whirling." He feels low and discouraged. Last week, as he talked of being low, you saw tears in his eyes although he controlled himself with some effort. He says that he is afraid that he is going to "lose it" if something does not change soon.

Write down how you might help Jim over the next few weeks. Include (a) anything else that you would like to know about Jim, especially what you would ask him the next time you talk, (b) what you think his biggest problem(s) is (are), (c) how you would like Jim to think about his problem(s), (d) what goals you might have for him, (e) what you would try to get him to do about his problem(s), (f) how you might accomplish this and (g) how you would know whether you were successful at helping him.

Helping Jim
Now that you have completed your study of Jim, let me share some observations that I make in our workshops. When I ask people what they would like to ask Jim, typically, they want to know about Jim's childhood, his friends, his devotional life and other information about possible *causes* of his problems. In fact, one point of this exercise is to see that there are many different ways to think about what is causing Jim's problems and that most people know a lot about helping already. The goal of this book is not to teach you how to discover the "real" cause of someone's problem—I believe that many problems have more than one cause. My purpose is to give you an overall

view of how people help others, regardless of the specific problems or causes.

Preoccupation with finding the "real" cause of emotional problems leads to the second point of this exercise. Most people are impatient when they begin to help someone else. Knowing only two paragraphs of information about Jim, people want immediately to test their theory about the cause of Jim's problems. When a professional counselor reads about Jim, a multitude of questions enters his or her mind. The questions do not revolve around the idea of cause; rather, they focus on *the problem's severity and duration*. For example, here are questions I might ask Jim at our next meeting:

1. Exactly how much are you harassed at work, and how ɹo you react to it?

2. What kind of pressure is your girlfriend putting on you? Can you withstand the pressure?

3. How frequently do these sins bother you? How much do they bother you? What specific circumstances provoke you to sin? What is your sexual sin?

4. How nervous or scared are you? What are you afraid of, and in what recent situations have you been afraid? What happens when you get nervous and scared?

5. How long have you had these symptoms of depression— poor appetite, loss of sleep, worry, feeling low and crying? How severe are the symptoms? How much do they bother you?

6. What does it mean for you to "lose it"? What change would prevent your losing it?

Only when I have decided the severity of the problems would I begin to investigate the cause. Patience is vital to helping.

Next, the questions you ask Jim about the cause of his problems will have a lot to do with how *he* thinks about his problems. Many inexperienced helpers lack a systematic plan for counseling; consequently, their questions lack direction and might confuse their friend. I tell beginning graduate students in counseling that they must have a plan when they enter a counseling session. As they listen to a client they might discard the plan after the first few minutes, based on new information, but they should start with a general plan.

I hope that this exercise has been useful to you, and that reading this book will help you to help friends more efficiently and effectively. Of course, reading this book will not make you a professional counselor. That takes years of education and supervised counseling experience. However, if you conscientiously learn the model, practice the skills and work through the applications, you will become a better counselor than you are now. And you will feel more confident the next time a friend asks for help.

Part I
A Model
for Helping

2
What Is
Christian Helping?

There are many Christian counselors, each with a different method. As we read their books and listen to their teachings, we must evaluate continually what they say they believe *and* how they actually behave during counseling. Not all counselors who say they are Christians counsel according to the biblical principles or even the moral guidelines that you might use. By comparing their beliefs with your beliefs, you can determine how much credence to give to their teachings. It is important for you to evaluate my beliefs about Christian helping, so I have placed this chapter early in the book.

Defining Christian Helping
Christian helping has four distinctives. It is done by a Christian. It is consistent with Christian assumptions. It has Christ at the

center. It is consistent with God's revelations.

I was visiting a church shortly after we had moved to Richmond. A woman (I'll call her Mary) asked me about my work.

"I teach counseling psychology at Virginia Commonwealth University," I replied.

"Oh, that's wonderful," she said. "We need more Christian psychologists."

I agree with Mary. We do need more Christian psychologists, for many Christians, when they have emotional problems, prefer to see Christian psychologists rather than psychologists who are not Christians. Mary thus used the most common definition of Christian psychology or of Christian helping: *it is helping done by a Christian.*

But this definition alone is not adequate. Many Christians who counsel people professionally do counseling that is indistinguishable from secular counseling. They love the Lord and live exemplary lives, but they counsel from a human-centered point of view without acknowledging the reality of the spiritual world and without making use of God's ability and willingness to heal people.

Thus, *Christian helping should be consistent with Christian assumptions.* But whose Christian assumptions? Most evangelical Christians, who believe that the Bible is the inerrant Word of God, believe that their assumptions are true. They do this even though equally fervent and devout evangelicals from other denominations believe opposite assumptions. Theologically liberal Christians might believe that their assumptions are the most useful or the most moral, but will not claim that their assumptions are absolute truth. In short, Christian assumptions differ, depending on which Christian is doing the assuming.

To me, Christian assumptions are the basic, core truths necessary to the Christian faith, as stated in the Bible and as practiced by Christians throughout the history of the church. These are clearly stated by C. S. Lewis (*Mere Christianity*) and by Francis Schaeffer (*The God Who Is There, He Is There and*

He Is Not Silent and *The Church before the Watching World*).[1]
These main Christian assumptions (see Table 1), affirm the
centrality of Jesus' resurrection whereby he conquered death
for those who establish a personal relationship with him as their
Savior and Lord.

Christians want Christ to be the center of their every activity.
Yet sometimes we fail. Having Christ as the center means being
guided and empowered by God's Holy Spirit, recognizing the
internal and external leading that God gives us. Having Christ
as the center also means reflecting the character of God in all
that we do. We must communicate with him and fix our minds
upon him, being ever mindful (that is, with our minds full) of
his presence and of his work in our lives and the lives of others.

*Christian helping should be consistent with God's revela-
tions.* Christians know truth because God reveals it to them.
God communicates. He always has—even before he created
the world, when only God the Father, Jesus and the Holy Spirit
existed. Even then he loved and communicated within the
Trinity. So when he created people in his image, he made them
to also communicate and love. God then communicated with
them. At first he did so face to face with Adam and Eve. Even
after the Fall he communicated with people and gave them
his written words (the Scriptures). But people refused to seek
God. They instead adhered strictly to the written words. Jesus
came. He was the living Word (Jn 1:1, 14). He was truly God
revealed in a way that people could understand (J. B. Phillips
called Jesus "God focused").[2] When Jesus was resurrected
and ascended, he sent the Holy Spirit who lives in Christians
and continually reveals God's truth. These revelations are the
special revelations of God, which give us specific knowledge
of his will for our lives.

God gave another kind of revelation, however, one that
all people could observe and from which they could infer his
existence. This is called general revelation and consists of two
parts. First, he created the world to reflect his glory. It is impossible for a person to look at the natural creation and not

Table 1
Basic Christian Assumptions

---

1. God exists.

---

2. He created matter, the universe, the world and people.

---

3. People share part of God's character (including a moral nature, the ability to communicate meaningfully and the ability to make decisions with real consequences).

---

4. At some point in history, Adam and Eve disobeyed God. As a consequence the world and all people became abnormal, or bent, and were thus out of personal relationship with a perfect, holy, just, and loving God.

---

5. Because people were finite and fallen, they could not re-establish relationship with God.

---

6. Because God is not only perfect, holy and just but also loving, he became a man, Jesus. Jesus was killed and suffered separation from God the Father as a punishment for sins which he did not commit. Jesus conquered death, re-establishing contact with God.

---

7. Anyone who truly believes that Jesus took his or her punishment and rose from the dead can have a personal relationship with God (that is, can become a Christian). This requires accepting Jesus as the Lord (ruler, ultimate authority) of his or her entire life. God provides his Holy Spirit to help Christians with this task.

---

8. Christian living involves bettering one's personal relationship with God through Jesus with the help of the Holy Spirit. This life provides more freedom and joy, both now and forever, than life without the relationship. It also demands responsible loving of other people.

---

9. Some day Jesus will return to earth and ultimately the old earth will be destroyed and replaced with a new earth.

---

know that there must be a Creator. Yet, when people harden their hearts (that is, when they presuppose that God does not exist) they fail to believe their eyes. Second, God created humans and gave them qualities that are shared by no other part of creation. The uniqueness of humans is a continuous testimony to the Creator in whose image we have been made. We have sciences which study general revelation. Even though many have forgotten the Christian assumptions upon which science is based, they still discover truths about God's natural creation. The natural sciences (such as physics, chemistry, biology, geography and astronomy) study the natural world, and the social sciences (such as psychology, sociology and anthropology) study the uniqueness of people.

I believe that what God has revealed—both his general and special revelations—is available for our use as Christian helpers. Therefore I believe that psychology, as a science, has some truths to tell us about helping. Furthermore, many of these truths will not be found in his special revelations, although they definitely should be consistent with the special revelations. The special revelations hold a position above the general because they are more clear and specific. We must always interpret the general revelation in light of the special, and not vice versa.

Of course, not all Christians share this view of the blending of biblical truth and psychological truth. In fact, some believe that psychology has little to offer the Christian helper. Others believe that psychology and the Bible should be kept separate. Still others believe that truths from each are equally valid. My view is that truths from each are equally valid if, and only if, the findings of psychology are consistent with the higher truths of God's special revelations.

Christian helping, therefore, *is helping that is done by a Christian who adheres to Christian assumptions, who relies on Christ as the center of the helping relationship and who uses whatever knowledge God has revealed.* Be aware that not every Christian does Christian helping.

Keeping on Track

Based on these ideas, here are some guidelines for helping. First, be sure that you are in a right relationship with God. This includes not only accepting that Jesus died to redeem you from the punishment you deserve because of your moral imperfection but also following Jesus as the sole guiding force in your life.

Second, get to know God more each day and learn to hear what he is saying. This means that you must talk to him as well as listen to the things that he tells you through the Holy Spirit and through reading and studying the Bible. Both sources of knowledge of God work together and do not contradict each other, yet the written Word of God is, in a sense, more reliable simply because it is permanent. When the Bible as we know it was constructed (or "canonized"), God spoke to the church fathers at the Council of Carthage (A.D. 397) and established the written Word as the standard of truth. (In fact, the word *canon* means "cane" or "rod of measurement.") Therefore, we can stay on track by adhering to the central truths of God's Word as interpreted by the wisdom of the ages.

Third, we can keep on track as Christian helpers by being affiliated with a local body of Christians in which we can effectively minister. One of my former pastors, Jerry Rouse of Columbia, Missouri, often said, "God didn't make Lone Ranger Christians." The way of the cross is both vertical toward God and horizontal toward others.

Fourth, remember that peripheral issues over which denominations have formed are more ambiguous and should be embraced tentatively. If you stress the central tenets of Christianity and remain tolerant on the others, you will avoid many theological debates which do not contribute to effective helping. C. S. Lewis, in *Mere Christianity,* explains,

> Ever since I became a Christian, I have thought that the best, perhaps the only, service I could do for my unbelieving neighbours was to explain and defend the belief that had been common to nearly all Christians at all times. I had more

than one reason for thinking this. In the first place, the questions which divide Christians from one another often involve
points of high Theology or even of ecclesiastical history which
ought never to be treated except by real experts. . . . And
secondly, I think that we must admit that the discussion of
these disputed points has no tendency at all to bring an out-
sider into the Christian fold. . . . Finally, I got the impression
that far more, and more talented, authors were already en-
gaged in such controversial matters than in the defense of
what Baxter calls "mere" Christianity.[3]

Probably the greatest weakness of evangelical Christians who
help others is that they often firmly believe that they are absolutely right in all areas. As a consequence they cannot abide
differences of opinion. Of course, not all evangelical Christians
feel this way, and they are not the only ones who feel this way.
But because we believe in absolute truths, we tend to err toward
rigid dogmatism more frequently than many others.

To combat this tendency we must acknowledge our finite-
ness and the resulting limits of our understanding. Imagine
a block of wood with a cross-shaped notch cut into the top of
it (see Figure 1a). Let this represent Christian truth. Each person, however, has only one perspective on truth. A person
viewing the block from the top would emphasize the cross
(Figure 1b). A person viewing the block from the bottom might
emphasize the firmness of the basis of truth (Figure 1c). Someone viewing the block from the end or from the side might
talk about depth of the Christian commitment (Figures 1d and
1e). No one could see the wholeness of the truth because truth
is infinite but we are finite.

Christian counselors, too, present limited perspectives.[4]
Each claims to do Christian counseling and each, because he
is finite, views this from a limited perspective. Lawrence Crabb
stresses deviation from Christian assumptions as the cause of
problems. Jay Adams stresses sin as the cause of all problems,
and he uses confrontation as the main intervention technique.
Clyde Narramore and Gary Collins are both eclectic in their

Figure 1
Limited Perspectives of Truth: An Analogy

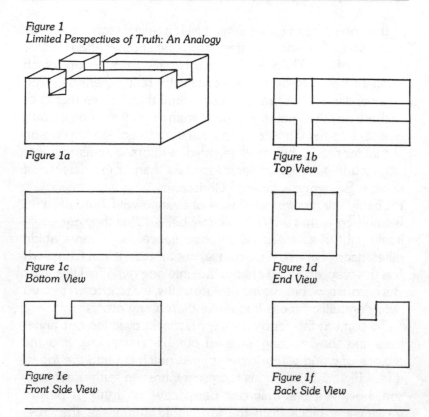

Figure 1a

Figure 1b
Top View

Figure 1c
Bottom View

Figure 1d
End View

Figure 1e
Front Side View

Figure 1f
Back Side View

approaches but not as systematic as some of the others. Paul Tournier stresses personal relationships as the key to healing. Tim LaHaye stresses the notion of temperaments as the cause of problems. John Powell is psychodynamic in his approach. Each man presents a different conception of Christian counseling and can help different people with his approach.

Be alert to a pitfall: don't think that you are always right and must "straighten out" the person that you are trying to help. Also, don't think that there is only one approach to Christian helping. In order to be a good helper, you must learn what other helpers have to teach you but not be content simply to copy them. You should expose yourself to many different helping styles and try out different ideas. See what works for you. As you mature as a helper, you will develop a style which is uniquely your own.

As Gary Collins recommends, Christian helping should be vitally concerned with making disciples. This means that through your help, people should come to love and trust the Lord more. Usually, you can indirectly disciple people by helping them solve their problems by using a Christian viewpoint. Properly done, this will help people grow closer to the Lord and will teach people that love is at work in the Christian community. And it might even help people avoid similar problems in the future, have insights about their problems and put these insights into concrete action.

This book provides one point of view. I will describe helping tools and general plans for using those tools with people who have a variety of problems. You will use your knowledge of the Bible and your unique relationship with Jesus when you practice using the tools and plans that I suggest. Then, through your own experiences, you will become a more effective helper.

3

What Are People Like and What Causes Problems?

Sue is often depressed. Her husband, Bill, works long hours as a salesman and has little time for the family. Sue's teen-age son is rebellious, frequently disobeying her in subtle, indirect ways. Her younger son is having trouble with school and wants only to play football, basketball or baseball, whichever is in season. Due to financial pressures, Sue and Bill decided that Sue needed to work part-time as a secretary. The only job she could find was as a legal secretary, and she has struggled to type the unfamiliar words without mistakes. Sue feels as if she is continually behind in her housework and at her job. Bill complains frequently that Sue is letting the house run down. Sue cries and thinks of the many troubles and pressures she faces.

Why is Sue depressed? What makes her take on so many responsibilities? Why can she not control her children? What is it about Sue that makes it difficult for her to confront her husband?

Personal Theories about People

Every person has a "theory" of personality; that is, every person has built from his or her experience a mental picture that describes what people are like and why they behave as they do. Often the picture is like a partially constructed jigsaw puzzle. The border is intact and describes how people generally behave: Are they good? Are they evil? Are they salvageable? This rough world view sets the stage for how we act toward others. We predict how others will act and try to act in a way that will influence them to behave as we want.

In addition to the borders, small puzzle-islands are relatively intact, yet the relationships among different portions are sometimes unclear. There are always some pieces of the jigsaw puzzle of life with which we are quite unfamiliar. Like seemingly unrelated puzzle-islands, our behavior differs according to the situation. A person who watched me play a hard, competitive game of racketball might not understand how I could talk sensitively with a client about deeply personal concerns or how I could lecture animatedly to college students. Because we behave differently in different situations, psychologists have been unable to describe personalities in a way that will help them predict what most people will do most of the time.

On the other hand, God gave humans a desire for order in their minds. As a result most people have a simplified picture of the world which describes both how the world operates and how people behave. This mental model helps us decide what to do in many different situations. With no model to predict the consequences of our behavior, we would be awash in a sea of uncertainty. We experience this in a limited way when we visit other cultures, especially Asian cultures which differ substantially from our own.

This chapter presents a simple model of people and problems on which this book is based. The model is gleaned from a study of God's revelations and, of course, from my experiences. I have tried to use Scripture as the standard of measurement and use psychology as a source of hypotheses about people. This model is not presented as the last word in counseling; it is intended merely to be useful to a helper.

Needs and Goals

What do you need to live? Food, air, water and shelter come immediately to mind. Yet those bodily and physical needs merely scratch the surface of human needs. The psychological needs must also be fulfilled to give us depth as people. Among other things, we need order, justice, stimulation, love, esteem and aesthetic appreciation. Three needs are particularly crucial to people who have problems: meaning, intimacy and responsibility.

Victor Frankl has built an entire counseling theory on the human need for meaning.[1] Erich Fromm believes that people cannot be "sane" without attributing their worth to something greater than themselves.[2] Many philosophers have also noted this need and have identified various objects that they think give meaning to life. Francis Schaeffer, who has critiqued many philosophical searches for meaning in his books, shows that attempts to find meaning without God are doomed to despair.[3] Only when God fills a person's life with the Holy Spirit can he or she experience the true meaning that gives the peace that passes understanding. This peace comes to us by snuggling ever closer into the arms of our Savior, trusting him more and more. People are created to continually pursue meaning and peace.

People also need intimacy. We were created to be in relationships—to love, to be loved, to be secure. We struggle to develop intimate relationships with others and with God. It is a labor of love, but it requires effort.

Third, people need to be responsible. They need to make real choices that have real consequences. God wants us always to choose to love and trust him. He wants us to be self-controlled (that is, controlled by our new self). We are called to make responsible choices moment by moment.

Our needs are never met totally because we live in a "bent" world. The world became abnormal when Adam and Eve elevated their needs for responsibility above their needs for meaning and intimacy by willfully disobeying God. Since then, people have continued to try to meet their needs in our fallen world by relying on themselves and other people rather than by relying on God (Rom 1:23). Such attempts never work. Our needs can only be adequately met through re-establishing contact with God, which is only possible by knowing Jesus personally. But note that even Christians have unmet needs because knowing someone takes time. A right relationship with God is like marriage. First, Jesus' Holy Spirit "courts" us, seeks us out, establishes contact, and convinces us by his love and by our inadequacy that we need him. Second, we marry Jesus, becoming the bride of Christ in a one-time event. Our justification (our acceptance of our proper relationship with Jesus) legally makes us his bride. If a marriage ended with the ceremony, however, few people would marry. In fact, what the ceremony dramatically does end is our life of self-sufficiency, and what it begins is a loving relationship that continues day by day. Our marriage with Christ, though—like human marriage—may not always be smooth. The love of married couples, like a muscle, often grows stronger through overcoming stress. In much the same way, as our relationship with Christ grows stronger, our needs are more fully met. Finally, though still remaining fully ourselves, we will become truly one flesh with Jesus. Our needs will be met, and we will be what God created us to be. But as humans who are not yet glorified, whether or not we are Christians, we are needy people. We try to meet our needs by relying either on Jesus or on ourselves. We always feel the tension of unmet needs and continually strive to reach the goals we set. The goals might or might not please God; nonetheless, we are goal-seeking beings.

Have you ever thought how dull life would be without goals?

What would we do all day? Yet by having a goal that we seek but do not yet accomplish, we feel tension or stress. People usually think of stress as undesirable, but God has created us so that we need some stress. With C. S. Lewis, I believe that we may even experience this in heaven. In *The Last Battle,* the final volume of The Chronicles of Narnia, and *The Great Divorce,* Lewis portrays heaven as always "further up and further in."[4] Heaven will definitely not be boring. We will have the perfect amount of stress. On earth, of course, we do not often experience this, and when we have either too much stress or too little stress we feel distress.

The Whole Person
When we are in distress, our entire being reacts. More than that, our friends and family get involved and our whole world changes. God made the whole person, and God made the person whole. It is impossible to be upset over some problem emotionally without involving the rest of our bodies. God created us to act as a whole unit, even making provision for the whole person to be redeemed, including giving us a new body. God also created us (in his image) to think and understand and simplify our experience. One way to do this is to look at only one part of our experience at a time. We may label these parts in various ways—such as heart, will and mind—depending on what we are trying to understand at the time. Each term is used in the Bible to tell us true things about people. Yet we must resist the temptation to think of people as separate parts enclosed within the skin. The different ways of "dividing" the person are merely useful ways in which God tells us something about the whole person.

Imagine that I baked a layer cake. The cake has a layer of white cake, then some white icing. On top of that is cherry cake, topped with cherry icing. On top of that is chocolate cake. The entire cake is covered with chocolate icing. There are various ways to talk about the whole cake. If I discuss the importance of the icing, I talk of the white, cherry and chocolate icings and the function of each. If I discuss the recipes I used to make the cake, I point out the different ingredients used to make each layer. Finally, we may want to eat the cake, so I can talk about the many ways of cutting the cake. I can cut thin triangular pieces, round pieces or large square pieces. I can cut the cake laterally through the center so that you get the entire chocolate layer and half of the cherry layer and I get the white layer and half of the cherry layer.

In the same way, there are many ways of talking about the parts of a person. How do I decide which way to "break the person into pieces"? I talk about the parts of people that communicate my point. I have found it useful in counseling to think of six areas of people's lives. People have a *spirit*. They need direct contact with God in a personal way. Without this contact, they are impoverished. People have *thoughts*. God created people to think words and, thus, communicate with him, with others and with themselves. People have *imaginations*. They see mental pictures. This helps some people remember life experiences more easily than remembering word labels for the experiences. People have *feelings*. Feelings are the punctuation marks of life. They make experiences exclamation points, commas, periods and even question marks. They help people interpret the meaning of their experiences. People make *actions*. They do things, and how they behave strongly influences their lives. Furthermore, people cannot not behave. They are always doing something (even if they are sleeping), and the choices they make are important. People have a *body*. They respond physiologically to their thoughts, images, behaviors, emotions and spirits.

Each of the six parts of a person is connected to every other part. It is as if all were joined by springs. Vibrations in one area of life will eventually set the others in motion also. Not only do people behave as a whole, but also the social and physical world of the person may be disturbed (see Figure 2).

For example, Beth fails several times to reach goals she has established. Before long she considers herself a failure. She

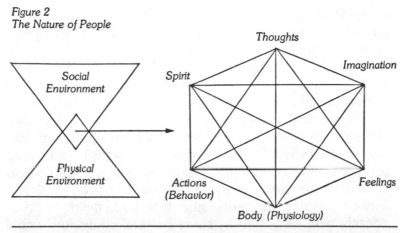

Figure 2
The Nature of People

thinks, "It's hopeless. I'm always going to fail. I'll never succeed. I'm no good." She imagines the worst, failing and being laughed at. She imagines herself unable to accomplish anything. She often cries and feels sad. She withdraws from her friends, feeling that she "would just depress them if I were around." When they invite her to a movie, she refuses because she does not feel like it. Neglecting the housework and her personal appearance, she soon allows her environment to become as cluttered as her thoughts. She stops her daily Bible readings and no longer feels like praying. Soon she even stops attending church. Because she does not have the energy to shop for groceries, she changes her eating habits. She loses weight, has elimination problems and often feels dizzy. Her sleeping habits change; she often has trouble getting to sleep at night and awakens before dawn. To compensate, she takes frequent naps in the morning and afternoon.

Beth's life is in disarray. Her whole life is involved, as is her physical living environment and her relationships with friends. If you were one of Beth's friends, you would want to know what is wrong. Why is she so troubled? Depending on your ideas about people and what causes problems, you would have some guesses. Let's look at what counselors might pinpoint as the cause of Beth's troubles.

1. Spiritual life. Spiritual approaches focus on three causes of human suffering: sin, self and Satan. For example, Jay Adams would say that sin was the root of Beth's problems.[5] He might say that failure itself was not her problem but that she had responded sinfully to her failure. He would identify various sinful behaviors and attitudes and admonish Beth to put off her old nature and put on her new nature. On the other hand, Lawrence Crabb would lay the blame for Beth's problems with her self. He believes that people have problems because they use nonbiblical thinking to satisfy their needs. Crabb would show Beth how she was trying to satisfy her need for significance by worldly successes rather than by bettering her relationship with God. Finally, some pastoral counselors would point out that "we are not contending against flesh and blood, but against the principalities, against the powers, against the world rulers of this present darkness, against the spiritual hosts of wickedness in the heavenly places" (Eph 6:12). Beth's problems might be viewed as Satanic attack. Sin, self and Satan *may* be collaborating to cause Beth's problems. Many other causes, however, may exist.

2. Thoughts. A number of counselors would conclude that Beth's thoughts were causing her problems. For example, psychologist Albert Ellis believes that people have problems because they have adopted "irrational ideas" with which they continually program themselves.[6] These irrational ideas lead to faulty emotions and behavior. Another psychologist whose reasoning is similar to Ellis's is Aaron Beck, who believes that people think "automatic thoughts" which keep them depressed.[7] Victor Raimy believes that people like Beth have problems because of "misconceptions of the self"; that is, people misunderstand themselves and their place in the world and thus have problems.[8]

3. Imaginations. Two well-known psychological approaches lay the blame for problems at the doorstep of imagination. Transactional Analysis, developed by Eric Berne and furthered by Thomas Harris and Claude Steiner, states that people develop a "picture" of their future, similar to the script of a play, which the person acts out.[9] Inevitability taints the script, like a Greek or Shakespearean tragedy which ominously marches to its foregone conclusion. A similar approach is that of Carl Rogers, who believes that people have an idea of their ideal self to which they never quite measure up.[10] The discrepancy between the real and ideal self results in anxiety and leads to other problems.

4. *Feelings.* Sigmund Freud would probably believe that Beth's problems were due to her unconscious, emotional conflicts.[11] She cannot express directly the anger she feels toward others. (Freud would look to Beth's childhood relationships with her parents for the reason for this inability to express anger.) Because Beth cannot express her anger directly, she expresses it indirectly by becoming angry with herself. This self-directed anger causes her depression.

5. *Behavior.* Behavior therapists would say that Beth's problems are caused by her behavior.[12] They would search for things Beth was doing that were not helpful and for things Beth was not doing that would have been helpful. They would try to discover conditions under which Beth could re-establish behavioral self-control over her life. They would help Beth learn to be her own counselor and to control her own behavior rather than to have her depression control her.

6. *Physiology.* Many psychiatrists and other physicians might view Beth's problems as the result of an upset body chemistry. They might recommend exercise and diet control if the problem were mild, a prescription to restore hormonal inbalances or psychoactive drugs to restore her brain chemistry. In some cases, they might even hospitalize Beth and recommend electroshock therapy.

7. *Social environment.* Jay Haley is a family therapist.[13] He might describe Beth's problems in terms of how her disturbance is related to her family. He might point out that Beth's parents were considering a separation when she became depressed but decided to stay together so that they would not further

upset Beth. Haley might also note the relationships between Beth and the members of her church. Her Bible study support group was able to rally around her, fostering a unity it had seldom achieved before.

8. Physical environment. Behavior therapists would conceptualize Beth's problems in terms of her environment as well as her behavior. They may point out how Beth's crowded, messy apartment may "cue"—like a cue card in a play—her to be depressed. They may also observe that Beth seldom has any pleasure because she has been "too tired" to have fun.

Who is right? What *really* is Beth's problem?

Actually there is *no one correct answer.* All the ways of thinking about her problem are correct to the extent that evidence can be found in Beth's life to support them. And evidence *can* be found because Beth is a whole person and her whole life is upset. Each way of thinking about Beth's problem will lead to a different proposed solution. This leads to the acid test of a helper's understanding of a problem: does it result in an effective solution? Even so, well might we wonder, How can the many therapies, which differ so greatly, be equally effective? Traditionally, psychologists have thought that despite their differences counselors do many things alike. Another possibility, however, is that people are complex and interconnected. There are many ways to think about problems; therefore, there are many ways to help people.

If there are many useful ways to think about problems, then we as helpers must sort through them. We also must decide how to effectively enter the life of the help seeker. The following chapter uses the model of people and problems discussed in this chapter to develop a way to enter the life of a person needing help. Then we can systematically help the person solve his or her problems.

4
Solving
Problems

What happens when a person develops a problem? What makes it worse? What can be done to solve the problem? What can a helper do to help a friend solve a problem quickly?

To answer these questions we will look at how Jesus helped the people he met and then at how scientists solve problems. Finally, I will introduce a five-step method of helping, which will be expanded in part two. This method will be applied to the various styles of several Christian counselors to show how they use it.

Many Doors
Your friends David and Suzanne Johnston ask for help with their six-year-old daughter, Lee. They have just had a conference with Lee's teacher, who thinks Lee is hyperactive. She

continually moves around the classroom, disrupting the other children. She has always been very energetic but this has recently become a source of some tension at home, where Lee often disrupts mealtime by jumping down from the table. Her parents often argue about her discipline. What would you recommend to David and Suzanne? There are many things they might do. Hyperactivity in children has been successfully treated by educators, psychologists, parents and physicians.

Suppose that David and Suzanne consult their family physician. Dr. Smith prescribes a well-known drug for Lee. What happens when Lee begins to take this drug? First, her brain is stimulated by this chemical, which in turn changes her thoughts. Instead of a moderately active thought life, Lee's mind begins to race. She is more excited about what she is thinking, so she does not act disruptively as often in order to keep herself excited. Lee begins to think, "My pills keep me calmed down. I am in control now. I feel a lot better now that I am taking my medicine." Because she feels more in control, Lee provokes her parents less. Her parents respond less authoritatively and even reward her more. They no longer call her a "problem child" or "hyperactive." Mealtimes become pleasant family times. Sunday mornings are not embarrassing, and David and Suzanne resume church attendance which they had discontinued after Lee's Sunday-school teacher complained about her "high energy level." In short, Lee has been greatly helped by treatment of the hyperactivity as a medical problem.

In contrast, suppose that Lee has been taken to a psychologist instead of the family physician. The psychologist conceptualizes the problem as "too much disruptive behavior" and teaches David and Suzanne ways to discipline Lee that are more effective than their methods. They begin disciplining Lee quickly and consistently after she misbehaves. They also reward her for eating complete meals without getting down from the table. In addition, they show Lee how to solve problems methodically and how to stop jumping from activity to activity. Dramatic changes occur in the Johnston family. The parents think, "We know how to help Lee. We know what we can do to keep her from misbehaving and to help her pay attention at school. We feel more in control than we did when this problem of hyperactivity came up." Lee might say to herself, "This is more pleasant than before. I know what I can and can't do. Mom and Dad are a lot nicer to me than they were before, and school is more fun now too." Meals also become more pleasant. In fact, Lee's changed environment and changed thinking actually change her brain chemistry without using drugs. David and Suzanne feel confident enough in Lee to return to Sunday school and church with her. In short, Lee has been greatly helped by treatment of the hyperactivity as a behavior problem.

Which method was better? Both methods worked. Very similar changes in the lives of the Johnstons could be produced by thinking about the problem of hyperactivity in very different ways. Why? Because, as we discussed in chapter three, people are whole people who are intimately related to their environments. Knowing that there are many ways to think about problems can comfort a helper, but with many doorways to a person's life, how do we know which is the best?

When Jesus encountered friends in need of help, how did he help them? Consider his concern for his disciples. Jesus did not pray, "Dear God, zap my disciples and make them powerful witnesses for you and give them instant belief in my deity." Instead he formed a close, personal and unique relationship with each. Relationships are the essence of Christianity—our relationships with God the Father, Jesus and the Holy Spirit, and our relationships with people, both Christians and non-Christians. *The first step in helping is being sure you have a personal relationship with the person you are helping.*

According to Erich Fromm in *The Art of Loving,* when we love someone, we *know* them, *care* for and about them, *respect* them and are *responsible* to them.[1] Each attribute of love requires daily "maintenance." For example, being responsible to a person means being "response-able"—able to respond

to the person's needs as they arise. This immediate responsive-
ness to the uniqueness of a person and to his or her needs char-
acterizes Jesus' helping relationships. In *The Sane Society*
Fromm suggests that *commitment* and *risk* are necessary for
a love relationship in addition to knowledge, care, respect and
responsibility.[2] If we are to help like Jesus, who is the embodi-
ment of love, then we must risk ourselves. We must be willing
to commit ourselves and our energy to helping and befriending
one in need.

Although Jesus was ultimately concerned with a person's
relationship with God, he did not always use their sin, their
faith or other so-called spiritual topics to gain entrance into
their lives. Sometimes he healed physical ailments (Jn 5:2-9);
sometimes he cured madness (Mk 5:1-20); sometimes he dealt
directly with sin (Mk 2:4-12). He preached. He taught. He
worked miracles. Sometimes he dealt with thoughts (Mt 5—7);
other times, he admonished people to behave differently (Mt
7:21-27). Jesus was compassionate, concerned with the whole
person, willing to help in whatever area the person was receptive. He told God's message of love and justice by how he acted
and by what he said. Jesus entered where the person expressed
a need. He entered by the open door. But first, he knocked
(Rev 3:20). When he was invited into the person's life, then
he entered.

What can we learn from Jesus? First, he dealt with people
as whole people who had many-faceted lives. Because each
person was whole, a disturbance in one area opened the door
to other areas. In our helping, then, if we are to follow in Jesus'
steps we must try to understand our friend's needs. We commit
ourselves to the person and treat him or her with knowledge,
care, respect and responsibility. We knock respectfully at the
door, then enter when we are invited.

Second, Jesus was flexible enough to intervene in others'
lives in many ways. He did not always treat a problem as if it
were caused by sin. He understood individual needs and the
approach to which a person would respond. For example, he

talked theology with Nicodemus, the Jewish scholar (Jn 3:1-15) but stressed self-denial with the rich young man (Mk 10:17-22).

Finally, Jesus sought to bring people into the full life that John 10:10 describes, which could be obtained only through submission of the whole person to God. To accomplish this, Jesus redefined the person's problem as one of spiritual need at the time most likely to be successful. He provided a new way of approaching problems that gave the person alternatives to do, think about, imagine and feel. We too must be alert to helping a person gain new perspective that will lead to new actions.

The second step in helping, then, is providing a new and useful way of viewing problems.

To better understand the necessity of and the power that comes from rethinking a problem, observe a scientist at work. Scientists deal with problems formally in much the same way the rest of us deal with problems informally.

How Scientists Solve Problems

When you work on a jigsaw puzzle, you have an idea of what the completed puzzle should look like. Perhaps you have a picture on the box top or a board on which to construct the puzzle. First, you form the borders. Then you systematically examine the colors and shapes of the exposed outline and try to find a piece which fills the gap. You see a promising piece. You try it. Perfect! You have just completed a successful experiment. You try another. Alas, this piece does not fit exactly. Something is too big, too little or the wrong color, so you toss it back and try again.

Science works like that. Scientists have assumptions and methods. But if their assumptions are not true to God's creation, scientists may get surprising results. Science historian Thomas Kuhn labels these *anomalies,* experimental results that do not agree with theories.[3] To understand this, journey with me to the time of Sir Isaac Newton, a great scientist and mathematician (and also, by the way, a Christian).

Newton has recently proposed his universal theory of gravitational attraction. One implication is that if a ball is tossed into the air, it will fall back to earth. One day I decide to test the theory. I toss a ball lightly into the air. Instead of falling, however, it accelerates into space. What a surprise! What do I do? Denial is my first response: "No, I don't believe that really happened. It was a freak. Maybe I dreamed it. Maybe some wind blew it. Maybe. . . ."

But to be on the safe side I check again. I toss the ball into the air. It again accelerates—faster than the time before. (I immediately swear off science-fiction novels.) After several repetitions I try with fear and trepidation to publish my findings in a scientific journal. None of the journal editors believe me. Finally, after fifteen editors reject me, one of my professional enemies publishes my article under a column headed "This Week's Crazy Results."

My worst fears come true. I receive insulting letters from my friends and the entire scientific community laughs hysterically at the mention of my name. Finally, however, a young researcher becomes intrigued and sets out to show where I went wrong. When she duplicates my experiment, however, she gets the same results! Editorials begin to criticize my work (and perhaps my character, my mental status and my preference for M & Ms). Several researchers attempt to show that I am wrong. More duplications. Debate increases. People take sides in the controversy, with some scientists defending me and others attacking. Researchers all over the world try to find where and how I went wrong. Most of the research in the field is devoted in some way to this controversial, disturbing topic. Emotions are volatile. The field of physics is in crisis.

Three solutions are possible. First, someone might do an experiment that neatly resolves the stalemate without changing the basic assumptions about gravity. In that case, normal science will resume. Second, the scientific community might become emotionally exhausted, decide that it will not be able to solve the mystery with its present knowledge and call a halt to the debate. Future generations of scientists might or might not return to the problem. Third, someone may propose a radically new way of conceptualizing the entire field of physics. Kuhn calls this "putting on a new kind of thinking cap."[4] This is what happened when Einstein reconceptualized physics and solved a number of problems for which Newton's theories were inadequate. Einstein did not just add something to Newtonian physics, he destroyed it. He annihilated it. Instead of thinking of space, motion and time as absolute, as had Newton, Einstein proposed that only one physical phenomenon was absolute. The speed of light in a vacuum was absolute and all other physical phenomena were relative to it.

If a new way of understanding physics (or any science) is proposed, scientists in that field may or may not accept it. Many just entering the field will adopt the new way of thinking. Some established scientists would, in Kuhn's words, have "conversion experiences" and would adopt the new assumptions. A scientific revolution would occur (see Figure 3). Scientists who bring about scientific revolutions are usually those who are new to the field and can look at it without bias.

How People Solve Problems

Everyone forms assumptions about how life works. We may not be able to state our assumptions, but we act as if we know how and why people behave as they do. We also have developed ways that we use habitually to solve our problems; therefore, we engage in "normal science" in which we solve our daily problems. Sometimes we encounter a problem that we cannot easily solve, so we (like scientists) pay much attention to solving the problem. These problems, which Kuhn calls anomalies, I will call *personal problems*. Usually these problems are resolved through prayer, our own effort, and possibly through seeking and using advice from friends. Personal problems disturb us, interrupting our normal activities, but most of them soon disappear. Occasionally, a personal problem stubbornly resists our attempts at solution. We seek advice from others, and we use their suggestions. We ask

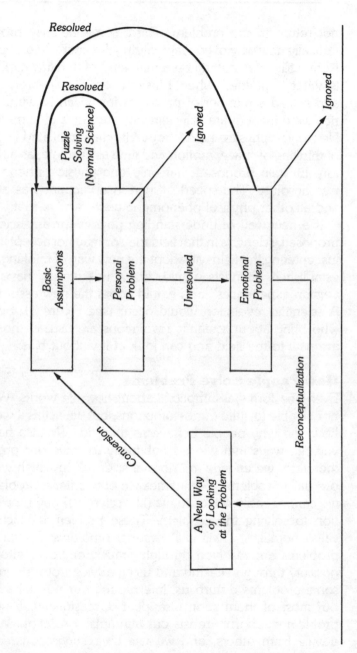

Figure 3
Problem Solving

friends and family to pray. We try everything we know, yet the problem persists. This persistent problem, a crisis in science, I call an *emotional problem*. Here are some of its characteristics:

1. Repeated attempts to solve the problem have failed.

2. Much advice has been sought, heard and tried, but without success.

3. Emotions are stirred up. People then overreact emotionally to small annoyances and disappointments.

4. People think they are losing control over their ability to cope with problems or even over their lives.

5. Relationships are disturbed as people try to control others because they do not believe they can control their own lives.

6. People think frequently about their problems, their lack of control, their depression and their catastrophic expectations.

7. People long to stop the distress.

8. People often blame themselves or others for their problems.

9. People's whole lives are affected.

Drawing from Kuhn's observations about scientists, we can see that there are three possible solutions to emotional problems. First, the person may resolve the problem without changing his or her understanding of it. This will not happen often. Usually common sense has been exhausted before the problem becomes an emotional problem. Also, the person will probably have been given much good advice already. Second, the person may put off the problem and then find later that it has vanished. Usually, however, the person cannot successfully use this "ostrich technique"—bury the head and hope the problem will go away. Third, the person may rethink the problem. This is the most common way and requires "putting on a new thinking cap," something very difficult for most people when they are emotionally involved in a problem. An objective person can help here. He or she has a different thinking cap and may be able to shed new light on the friend's problems.

Yet, discovering new ways of thinking about the problems

of a friend is not easy. How can we make this easier? When you listen to your friend tell about her or his problem, listen naively. Pretend that you do not know your friend. Listen as if you had just met the person. What is your friend leaving out of the story? What is assumed? Bringing out these assumptions often will provide a new way of thinking.

Systematically review the eight areas of a person's life and environment. Ask yourself questions about each area. For example, in the spiritual area, ask: Does the problem seem to be involved with sin, self or Satan? Or, concerning the thought life, consider: What thought patterns seem to make things worse? New ways of viewing the problem should emerge.

Remember that your goal is not merely to think about the problem in a new way. You are trying to think about the problem in such a way that the person will be able to try new solutions. One way to know whether you are helpfully conceptualizing a problem is to notice whether you are using a "be-verb" or an "action-verb." For example, if you say, "The problem is that John is lazy," then you used a be-verb *(is)*. This is likely to not be helpful because John cannot easily change the way he is. But John can change what he does. If you say, "John misbehaves," then you used an action-verb. This may lead to helpful solutions because misbehavior can be stopped by rewarding proper behavior and by punishing misbehavior. Why? The person needs to act in order to solve a problem. Merely thinking about the problem differently is not helpful. When the person acts differently, he or she can then find out what works and what does not work.

Stages of Helping
This look at the way Jesus helped people and at how scientists solve problems can help us develop a general model of how problems can be solved. This model describes what effective helpers do. It describes well the behavior of counselors, be they Christian or not.

The model has five stages. The first stage is *understanding the person* and has three steps: making sure the person feels understood, finding out what you need to know to describe the problem and finding which doorway will communicate your understanding. The second stage is helping the person *rethink the problem.* The third stage is *making an action plan* and includes planning a number of changes and motivating the person to carry out the plans. The fourth stage is *supporting the person's attempts to change.* The fifth stage is *following up* to see whether changes happened and how they worked.

Identifying separate stages of helping is, in a way, misleading, for Stage 1 (understanding) never really ends. You frequently recycle through the stages—strengthening the help seeker's conceptualization of the problem, refining action plans and following up each one to evaluate its effects, and offering support continually. But we will consider the stages separately to help you polish your skills in each stage.

I have presented a general helping strategy which does not say, "Quote Scripture here. Exhort here. Confess here." Your use of Scripture, exhortation, confession and other techniques will depend on the person, the problem and the situation. Furthermore, this plan describes how people act. It does not prevent the Holy Spirit from intervening powerfully in a situation; in fact, it provides a vehicle through which the Holy Spirit can work.

This plan is a map of the territory of helping. With a map, a person may navigate using many paths and roadways. Familiarity with major landmarks (stages) may make the navigation easier and more systematic. In part two of this book, I will sketch in the terrain around the major landmarks, discussing things you can do during each stage of counseling.

Part II
Skills of the
Effective Helper

5
Communication Problems (Stage 1)

The first stage of helping is understanding the person and expressing that understanding to the person. Because understanding depends on two-way communication, we must know the rudiments of communication before we help the person rethink the problem (Stage 2), make action plans (Stage 3) and carry them out (Stages 4 and 5). I am emphasizing the importance of Stage 1 by spending this chapter and the next four in discussing it.

Day after day we talk with people. We seem to understand and be understood. Friends and family often want to talk to us. Does this mean that we are good communicators? Perhaps, but we can all improve our talking and listening. Whether or not we are helping someone, we occasionally misunderstand and are misunderstood; therefore, in this first chapter on Stage

1 I will describe communication problems that cause misunderstandings. Then I will explain how helpers can avoid these problems, concentrating on power struggles.

Why Communicate?

People communicate to meet their needs and to influence others. The needs might be basic (such as food, water, security or love), or more specialized (such as a good self-concept, friendship, respect or enjoyment of a soothing piece of music). We usually try to meet these needs by asking for help, by doing something aimed at meeting our need or by manipulating others instead of asking directly. In short, we try to influence others. God has placed us in a world where our actions matter; consequently, we like to see the results of our actions. If we do not see effects, we become discouraged.

Being created in God's image means communicating. We cannot *not* communicate.[1] If my wife, Kirby, asks me a question and I do not answer, I have communicated nonetheless— perhaps that I don't care, that I am angry, that I am depressed or even that I did not hear the question. Regardless of content, though, I cannot avoid communicating something; even the simplest answer will transmit much information. Albert Mehrabian, a psychological researcher, has found that words are responsible for only seven per cent of the overall impression we give.[2] Thirty-eight per cent is due to voice quality—soothing, harsh, caring. Over half of the impression (fifty-three per cent) results from visual qualities such as facial expressions or body movements. The message is loud and clear. We continually communicate, whether we want to or not.

In the same way, we cannot *not* influence help seekers. Our attempts at helping, moreover, are not automatically successful because we care or because we mean well or even because we have successfully helped others with the same problem. Psychologist Hans Strupp puts it well when he says that helping is for better or for worse.[3] To help others we must systematically influence them, being aware of how and why we are doing it to achieve the goals that we and the other person have set.

Good and Bad Translations

Think about a time when you communicated well with someone. What happened? How was that different from the time when you just "didn't click" with someone else? What makes us understand each other better?

To answer these questions, consider this brief description of communication. Every communication effort has five parts: a sender, a receiver, a message, a context and feedback. The *sender* says and does something to the *receiver*. The *message* is formed by what is said and what is done. The *context* comprises what is happening while the message is sent and the memories of past communication attempts by the sender and the receiver. *Feedback* is what the receiver gives, in actions or words, in response to the message. Feedback indicates understanding or the lack of it.

Unfortunately, people don't always understand each other. Why does the receiver sometimes understand a meaning different from what the sender intended? The answer lies in how the sender says the message and what the receiver does with it.

The sender tries to send the message as clearly as possible, which is best done when the context, actions and words speak in unison. When any one of the three is out of sync with the other two, misunderstanding occurs. For example, after a hard day at work Frank collapses in the easy chair with a novel. "This was really a bad day," sighs Margaret. "Uh huh . . . tell me about it," mumbles Frank without glancing up. When she runs crying into the bedroom he looks up, puzzled. "What did I say?" he asks himself. Of course, it was not what he said that upset Margaret. Rather, she was upset because Frank's words and actions didn't say the same thing.

The sender can send hard-to-understand messages for other reasons. Expressing an experience in words is like translating a sentence from one language to another. Just as the two sentences are not the same, though they relate to the same idea or action, my experience is not the same as the words I use to talk about it. Something is lost in the translation. Of course, some translations will be better than others, and the meaning will change more or less depending on the translation's quality. If I say, "I moved," you can imagine an action I might have taken. Yet "I moved" is such a poor translation of my experience that your mental picture of my movement probably is not much like my actual movement. If I say, "I moved my hand" or, better still, "I moved my hand from the desk to my right pants pocket," you have a much clearer picture of my experience.

Richard Bandler and John Grinder applied these ideas to counseling and claimed that people with emotional problems often do not see the many ways they have to solve their problem.[4] For example, a man we will call Fearful is consumed with fear of failure and can act only terrified and defensive when it looks as if he will fail at a task. He cannot act differently because he sees only one option. If someone could help him see other options, however, he could be free from his irrational fear. The following conversation demonstrates how someone might make him aware of other options by helping fill in the missing and distorted information that results from translating experience into words.

Fearful I'm afraid. [This statement does not convey much information. A helper should try to help Fearful complete his picture of what is feared.]

Helper What are you afraid of?

Fearful I'm afraid of failing. [This answer is still incomplete.]

Helper You are afraid of failing *at everything?* Can you imagine anything at which you are not afraid to fail? [This question gently challenges Fearful's implication that he is afraid to fail at anything.]

Fearful Well, yes, there are some things.

Helper What's the difference between things that matter and things that don't matter? [This helps Fearful identify exactly what is important.]

Fearful For one thing, I don't want to fail at things that will hurt me or my family physically, emotionally or financially.

Helper Let's see... there must be many things that don't fit into those categories. Of course, no one likes to fail, but there is a big difference between being afraid of *any* failure and only being afraid of failures that harm you or your loved ones. [Much information about Fearful's fears is still unclear; more counseling could further sharpen his perception of his problem.]

In a brief communication the receiver usually has observed only a small bit of behavior—perhaps one sentence, a facial expression and a body position. Yet from that small transmission the sender expects the other person to get a great deal of information, including the correct interpretation of what was said, the emotional meaning, the motives of the sender, and even how the sender expects the receiver to respond. To accomplish this monumental task, people guess the meaning of a communication. The receiver continually compares his or her guess with the sender's message. Once the receiver makes a guess (and most people do this with amazing speed), the guess is not easily changed even if new information is added. People distort and ignore information to prove their guesses "correct." If the initial guess is fairly accurate, people may understand each other. If the initial guess is wrong, however, numerous misunderstandings may occur. Good communication depends on the accuracy of the guesses.

Weeding the Garden

"A weed," said my expert gardener of a neighbor, "is any plant, even a rosebush, that is growing where you don't want it to grow." Our helping efforts are sometimes teeming with verbal weeds which hinder fruit production in helping relationships. One reason for ineffective helping is our reluctance to carefully and systematically tend our gardens and remove unwanted communication techniques. (Chapter seven is devoted to weeding out these hindrances.)

A helper sometimes overreacts to requests for help: "Oh, dear. What will *I* tell her?" A minicrisis erupts in the helper, compounded by feelings that his or her basic rights have been violated; "Doesn't she know how busy I am? How can she expect me to spend so much time with her?" The helper might also feel inadequate to the task, overwhelmed by forebodings of failure: "What if I can't help? What if my mind goes blank?" If you are overconcerned with what you will say, you might communicate that you do not understand or, worse, that you do not care. In addition, when you are preoccupied with your own actions, you might give advice too quickly. Premature advice closes doors to further helping.

What makes for good communication in other conversation does not always transfer to helping situations. In fact, our conversation habits may interfere with helping. In regular conversations, for example, the focus of attention alternates between talkers, but in helping situations the focus of attention remains on the help seeker. Most of the conversation in the early stages of helping is aimed at understanding the help seeker's problems and at helping him or her think about those problems in a different way. After that, conversation is aimed at finding and evaluating possible solutions to those problems. In regular conversation, people often concentrate on being witty, entertaining, interesting and likable—in short, on themselves and the effect they are having. Consequently, we must use our communication skills differently and perhaps use new communication skills (see chapter nine).

Mary asks for help. Long silences punctuate the already sparse conversation. You are confused by apparently contradictory information from Mary. You don't know how to help. Mary begins to cry hysterically.

Jim asks for your help. You blunder through the conversation, embarrassed. You realize that you have forgotten to ask several important questions. Jim looks scornfully at you after a long silence, then rises and walks away, shaking his head.

Fantasies such as these dramatize another communication

concern. Most helpers, especially novices, experience such nightmares.[5] Such catastrophes rarely happen, though, because blunders can be easily corrected with experience and preparation. Furthermore, they seldom create rifts in relationships. Let's examine each blunder and plot our strategy.

1. Long periods of silence. Silence is not necessarily bad. People with emotional problems often have conflicting thoughts. Because it takes time to sort through the confusion, a person may pause before answering a question. Although this thinking time can seem embarrassingly long, help seekers are often unaware that they have taken a long time to answer.

2. Confusion. If you are confused, assume that the person seeking help is also. It is not wrong to express your bewilderment, saying, for example, "Excuse me, Mary, I am a little confused. Earlier I thought you said that you hated the extra work that Marvin had to do. But you just said that you could not do without all the money he earns. Can you clear this up for me?" This may help the person recognize his or her own unclear thinking. The attitude, conveyed by your tone of voice and expression, should be, "I really don't understand how you are seeing the situation."

3. Not knowing how to help. Your first goal is not to help but to understand the person. If you truly understand, you help by support, by encouragement and by your very presence. No one is expected to have all the answers—especially not before knowing what the problem is. What you are expected to have is a plan of action. You have that plan: listen and try to understand.

4. Overestimating blunders. Virtually all damages can be repaired later if you conscientiously try to understand the person.

5. Forgetting questions. Few questions are so critical that they must be asked at one and only one point in a conversation. Be sensitive to natural breaks in the conversation and say, for example, "Jim, I forgot to ask: When did you first begin to feel depressed?"

6. Negative evaluation. People who have emotional problems are usually so entangled in their own problems that they do not judge how well you are helping. They have much to ponder; criticizing you saps mental energy. Moreover, your friendship probably is not based on your helping skills. Helping is an extra dimension to most friendships. When you are asked for help, do not worry about how you will be evaluated. Focus on the main task, which is to understand what the other person is communicating.

Power Struggles

The most common communication difficulties, however, result from power struggles. In a helping relationship a power struggle is not usually crude bullying that results in head-to-head confrontation. In fact, it is almost imperceptible. People merely get hurt feelings, mumble to themselves that their rights have been violated, or seethe with anger and resentment. Atrophied communication is like a cold war in which people avoid each other, if possible. If not, they seek allies.

What causes power struggles? How might they arise in your relationship with a person who has a problem? What can you do if someone tries to enlist you as an ally in a power struggle? Because people in close relationships mutually influence each other, they develop unwritten rules which govern their relationship.[6] Most are unaware that their relationships obey rules, much less what the rules are. Such rules, however, come in three varieties.

The first type comprises rules well known to each member of the relationship. For example, Joe and Mary have an explicit agreement about who will empty the trash. They do not need to discuss this job because they know their responsibilities. People are not aware of the second type of rules, but would nonetheless agree if the rules were called to their attention. For instance, Ted and his wife, Kay, live by the rule that in a crisis he will turn to her for emotional support. The third type is composed of rules which people are unaware of and which they would not accept if made aware of them. These rules usually involve power in a relationship; for example, the Allen household is governed by the rule that in matters of discipline, the children control the family. Eighteen-month-old Kelly begins to eat dirt from the potted plants in the living room. Her mother yells at her to stop. The child ignores her and continues to shovel dirt into her mouth. Mother is exasperated—this is the fourth time in three days that she has found mud on Kelly's chin. She flies across the room and grabs the little girl by the arm, frightening her. Little Mud Mouth cries loudly; her mother yells even more loudly. Father, who has been trying to read in the den, wanders out and says, "Honey, don't you think you're overreacting? It's only a little plant. I'll get you another one on the way home from work tomorrow." The child runs to her father and hugs him affectionately. She looks accusingly over her shoulder at her mother and wipes her chin surreptitiously on her father's white shirt. Peace is restored, but at the cost of raw emotions and hidden resentment. Each plots what he or she will do the next time.

This power rule is the heart of most problems in relationships. They occur when one member of a relationship tries to change a rule and thus dashes the other's expectations or assumptions, especially those governing control of the relationship. People frequently define and redefine their relationships. When one person asks another to do something, the asker is defining (or redefining) the relationship as one in which such requests are appropriate. If one tries to redefine the relationship and the other resists, a power struggle ensues. The mark of a power struggle is that one or more people involved spend much time rehearsing future encounters and feeling that their rights have been violated. These struggles are common in three settings: families, employment situations and helping relationships.

Power struggles develop in helping relationships because a request for help changes the rules of the relationship (even if temporarily). In professional counseling, when a person asks for help he or she steps into a position of need. The entire purpose of the relationship is to provide help to the client. Although clients usually realize this, they often resist the counselor's suggestions. Helping relationships between friends, however, are less formal, so resistance is less. On the other hand, because friends need to maintain equality in the relationship, power struggles still exist. Both the helper and the help seeker will at times become emotional and rehearse their interactions. Learn to recognize the symptoms of power struggles so you can avoid them.

A power struggle with a friend will impair your effectiveness as a helper. Be alert also to the effect your help has on people other than the one you are helping. Perceived alliances can ensnare you in a power struggle. If Carol and Mike are having marital problems and you help Carol, then Mike might feel ganged up on. Well-intentioned alliances between friends are frequent: the friend, drawn unwittingly into a power struggle, usually feels "right" about providing support and, having heard only one side of the story, that the person seeking help has been "wronged." If Carol asks you for help, she puts you in a difficult position. Any time you deal with only one member of a relationship, you risk becoming part of an alliance, with or without giving your permission. How do counselors avoid this bind?

A professional counselor determines who is the client—in general, it is the person with whom he or she is talking. This principle may help you to help Carol and Mike. For as long as you are talking with Carol, she alone is your "client." You should urge *her* to talk with Mike about their problems. You should focus on what *she* can do to improve her home life. You should avoid siding with judgments such as "You are right and Mike is wrong." Rather, say that she should work out with Mike what is right for their particular situation. Then, after you have tried to help Carol with *her* responsibilities, prepare yourself for the possibility that Mike will come to you some day and say, "Carol said that you said. . . ."

Relationship problems are tricky. To assume that because

only one person asks for help, your help will only affect one person, is dangerous and naive. Whether (and whom) you will help depends on the circumstances. You might intentionally ally with one person. You might decline to help, believing that you would do more harm than good. Your decision of whether to help most likely will be governed by the relationship you have with both parties.

It Takes Time

When I took up tennis, I fell in love with the game. So after randomly pinging the ball around the court, I made a beeline for the public library and checked out every book about tennis that I could get my hands on. After much diligent study, careful reflection and mirror practice, I proudly strutted onto the court, armed with my Pancho Gonzales backhand, my Bjorn Borg forehand and my Jimmy Connors serve. I was ready for the world—but was the world ready for me?

In actual practice, my Pancho Gonzales backhand looked like that of Pancho Missbyamile (heavy on the *miss*). My Bjorn Borg forehand rarely connected, and my serve—well, after one week I was called D. F. (Double Fault) Worthington. But a book by Bill Tilden exhorted me to be patient. That encouraged me to continue to practice hitting the ball correctly rather than revert to my old unorthodox style which was better in the short run but had limited promise for the future.

Effective helping and effective tennis have something in common. When you pay attention to the individual parts of any complex skill, you will probably experience an initial period of awkwardness. So practice good communication: you will improve. Do not get discouraged if your helping feels awkward at first. Learning to help effectively takes time. Remember that for clinical and counseling psychologists to be licensed to see clients, they must complete four or five years of academic work combined with counseling experience, and then complete two years of full-time supervised counseling experience. Learning to help effectively takes time and effort.

6
Understanding Emotions (Stage 1)

The first stage of helping is to understand another person and the person's problems. To do this you must understand emotions. An emotional problem is one with strong feelings associated with it, be they close to the surface, bubbling up at the slightest provocation or rigidly controlled. Emotions are powerful. If not properly understood, they can lock a relationship into patterns of behavior that perpetuate the problem.

This chapter explains how emotions give information. I consider how to recognize the shades of emotion, to realize what emotions accomplish and to identify how people react to the different emotions. I also discuss how people keep their emotions private. Finally, I cover what to do when someone you are talking with becomes very emotional.

What We Learn through Emotions

Emotions are invaluable to planning a helping strategy and influence both partners in a relationship. Emotions give three kinds of information: the meaning of the problem to the person, the conflicts he or she is experiencing and the ways in which the person tries to solve problems.

The meaning of a problem. Emotions reflect and punctuate part of the truth of a problem. The problem is not found in the emotion itself, however, but in the person as a whole person. Emotions are not easily understood when we do not fully empathize with our friend. We may observe a person expressing an emotion and yet may not see the emotion. We must develop an "emotional world view" to discover useful information under the surface.

Psychologists disagree on the importance of emotions to counselors. Some believe that people have problems primarily because they do not handle their emotions well.[1] Others treat emotions as less than a central cause of emotional problems. Albert Ellis, for example, treats emotions as dependent on people's thoughts. For example, suppose you are driving in a city during rush hour. It is hot, and you have the windows rolled up because of a heavy rain. Suddenly a car directly in front of you stops and the driver, double-parking, rushes into a building. Of course, your car and many cars behind you are blocked. Horns blare. The heat rises in your car and with it, your anger. Suddenly the driver emerges from the building, carrying a young girl whose legs are paralyzed. Your anger subsides immediately. The situation is the same as it was before you saw the man carrying the girl. Yet now your anger is replaced by shame at your behavior and compassion toward the girl. Why did your emotion change? You thought different thoughts. Instead of thinking how hot it was and how inconsiderate the man was, you suddenly thought how tragic it is for such a young girl to be paralyzed. Your thoughts quickly changed your emotions. Ellis believes that thoughts always control emotions; consequently, thoughts are more important than emotions as causes for emotional problems. Behavioral counselors also have assigned a secondary role to emotions, believing that we learn to express our emotions in the same way we learn to do other things—by association.

Emotions serve many purposes. One is to communicate the meaning that events hold for us to the people who see our emotional behavior. What we communicate depends on our past experiences. For example, if Joan reacts to the death of her father by crying, publicly and privately, she may be communicating one or more of the following messages:

1. "My father was very important to me. See how severely his death affects me."

2. If she cries more in the presence of her family than in the presence of her close friends, she may be saying to her friends, "Sure I will miss my father, but I can cope."

3. "I never tried to get close to my father. Maybe if I cry loudly I'll drown my conscience."

One caution is in order. Though we may understand what a person's emotion means, we may choose not to bring that meaning to his or her attention. Emotions can be strong and frightening, and people often need to control them to tell themselves that they still have at least some control over their lives. It is not always an act of kindness to encourage the release of emotions. Do *not* adopt a general rule that says emotions should always be expressed. Try instead to uncover what the emotions mean to the person and then decide whether it would be helpful to encourage expression.

Conflict.   Understanding emotions can also unlock the door to conflicts. One of the best-known, most widely agreed upon psychological principles is that *people often are torn by conflict within themselves.* Human conflict permeates the Bible and tests the Christian at every turn: to follow God or Satan, to live by the Spirit or by the flesh, to obey or to sin, to live for Jesus or for self. The apostle Paul asked, "Why do I do the evil I don't want and leave undone the good that I do want?" (Rom 7:19, my paraphrase). He concluded that a principle which he did not consciously will was in conflict with his conscious will. He identified the principle as sin (v. 20).

Eighteen centuries later, Freud said that people behaved "irrationally" because they were controlled by their dynamic unconscious minds.[2] In saying this, he merely gave a new name to sin. He proposed that the unconscious mind includes the id, a repository of primitive urges and self-seeking desires (see 1 Jn 2:16), and the superego, a combination of a strict conscience and adopted values of the world (see Rom 2:15; 12:2). Since Freud, many psychologists have fleshed out the barebones picture that Paul presented of how sin, as an unconscious principle within us, causes conflict (see Table 2). Carl Rogers says that people do what they do not want to do because they have indiscriminately adopted the values of others.[3] B. F. Skinner claims that people do what they do not want to do because they have been rewarded for that behavior in the past.[4] Aaron Beck attributes this behavior to "automatic thoughts" and Albert Ellis says it is due to "irrational ideas." The constant theme is that conflict exists between the will of humans and the many-faceted principle of sin.

When we help a troubled and confused person, we want to understand his or her conflicts. Confusion is the blending together (fusing) of conflicting thoughts. Sometimes merely identifying clearly the opposing choices makes decision making easier. If helpers can recognize the subtle shades of emotion, they can feed back information that may help the person. For example, I once counseled a woman who needed to confront her roommate. For two weeks she procrastinated. As she described one opportunity she had passed up, her face registered fear. When I suggested that perhaps she was afraid that something terrible would happen if she confronted her friend, she burst into tears and told how her parents had harshly punished her whenever she had disagreed with them. After we discussed the appropriateness of these fears in the present situation, she was able to confront her friend effectively. She

Table 2
Conflict between Human Will and Sin

Author	What Makes Me Do What I Don't Want	Biblical Reference
Paul	Sin	"I do not understand my own actions. For I do not do what I want, but I do the very thing I hate. . . . Now if I do what I do not want, it is no longer I that do it, but sin which dwells within me" (Rom 7:15, 20).
Freud	Unconscious mind: id and superego (which includes conscience and introjected values)	"For all that is in the world, the lust of the flesh and the lust of the eyes and the pride of life, is not of the Father but is of the world" (1 Jn 2:16). ". . . their conscience also bears witness and their conflicting thoughts accuse or perhaps excuse them" (Rom 2:15b). "Do not be conformed to this world . . ." (Rom 12:2a).
Rogers	Adopting values of others	"Do not be conformed to this world . . ." (Rom 12:2a).
Skinner	Past learning; past rewards	"Learn not the way of the nations . . ." (Jer 10:2a).
Beck	Automatic thoughts	"For as he thinketh in his heart, so is he" (Prov 23:7 KJV).
Ellis	Irrational ideas	". . . for although they knew God they did not honor him as God or give thanks to him, but they became futile in their thinking and their senseless minds were darkened" (Rom 1:21).

confessed later that she had still been afraid but was able to confront because she understood why she was afraid. My identification of her emotion helped her identify her conflict.
Method of solving problems.   Because emotions communicate information, people use them to solve problems. For example, Mary is doing the dishes and thinking, "John's being unfair by watching TV while I have to work." Before long she is so upset that she begins to cry softly. John notices. With a sigh he rises and picks up a dishtowel. Mary has solved her problem by emotional communication. But if Mary and John continue to solve their problems by emotional rather than verbal communication, Mary could be plagued by depression and John by anger. Both would hate each other's behaviors but both would perpetuate the pattern because their emotions "solve" their problem.

The helper should be aware that when people express emotions, they are communicating something. The helper who is not aware of this may respond inappropriately. For example, Kate typically solves her problems by becoming angry. Her family and friends are well aware of her outbursts, and they carefully protect her from annoying circumstances. Gayle solves problems by fear. People protect her from things which may make her afraid. Frank becomes morose and depressed easily. His colleagues often do favors for him because they do not want little things to upset him. If you were a friend of Kate or Gayle or Frank, you may choose to help them in the same way others do—by protecting them. If you are aware of their patterns, however, you may want instead to help Kate learn to handle annoying circumstances or to help Gayle conquer her fear or to help Frank meet his responsibilities. You have the choice.

Recognizing Different Emotions
How do we distinguish among different emotions? According to William Hinds, there are eight primary emotions (see Table 3).[5] Each emotion ranges in intensity. For example, unhappi-

Table 3
Emotions: What They Look Like and What They Do

Emotion	What the Emotion Accomplishes	What Happens to the Person's Face	Emotional Responses Aroused in Helpers
distress-anguish	signals withdrawal for protection, asks for help	eyebrows down and together, forming "worry triangle"; cheeks stretched down; worry lines form	caring, fear
anger-rage	helps us get what we want, threatens people	mouth and jaw firmly set, lips thin, eyes narrowed, hard stare, squinting, snarling, lips back to show eye teeth	fear, distress, anger
fear-terror	protects us, gets us moving	whites show over eyes, eyebrows knitted, forehead wrinkled, mouth open	fear, contempt
guilt-shame	protects us, shows submission	head down, eyes down, flush, blush	shame, anger
disgust-contempt	repels or rejects (associated with smell or taste)	contempt: one corner of upper lip raised; disgust: both corners of upper lip raised	disgust, contempt
interest-surprise	focuses attention, orients us	interest: rapt attention, concentration; surprise: whites show over eyes, eyebrows raised, mouth open	caring, loving
happiness-joy	releases tension	smile, laugh, nostrils flared, cheeks raised, "crow's feet" form	happiness-joy
caring-loving	restores us, nurtures, cares, focuses us on things outside ourselves	"star gaze," look into other's eyes, "soft" eyes	caring, loving

ness ranges from distress (mildly unhappy) through anguish (deeply sorrowful). Other emotions extend from mild anger to rage, fear to terror, guilt to shame, disgust to contempt, interest to surprise, caring to loving, and happiness to joy. How can you recognize each emotion? When people experience emotion, their entire bodies are involved. When people are sad, their shoulders sag, their muscles relax, and their entire body slows down. Moreover, one part of the body is even more expressive—the face.

Distress-Anguish.   When Cain saw that he had not pleased God with his sacrifice, "his face fell" (Gen 4:5 NEB). What does a fallen face look like? The eyebrows are pulled down and together toward the bridge of the nose, forming a "worry triangle" just above the bridge of the nose. The corners of the mouth are pulled down. This flattens out the cheek muscles and gently stretches down the lower part of the eye. This, in turn, pulls open the tear ducts, making crying easier. Look into a mirror and think sad thoughts. Try to show sadness on your face. Observe how your face looks when you are sad. Observe others who are truly sad or are pretending to be sad.

Anger-Rage.   Anger most affects the mouth and eyes. The mouth becomes firm. The teeth are clenched, and muscles in the jaw sometimes bulge. The lips are often compressed and the person looks "thin-lipped." When anger turns to rage, the lips pull back from the teeth in a snarl. The mouth becomes square and the eyeteeth are usually visible. The eyes usually narrow when the person is mildly angry. The neck is thrust out slightly and the person appears to be staring hard. As anger grows into rage the eyes flash, opening wide, while the brows knit together.

Fear-Terror. A person who is afraid withdraws. The eyelids pull back, showing the white above the iris. At the same time, the eyebrows are pulled down at the bridge of the nose and are elevated in the middle. The forehead wrinkles. A terrified expression is an exaggeration of fear. The eyes open wider and the mouth also opens.

Guilt-Shame.   Guilt is very difficult to recognize. The most distinctive feature is a reluctance to meet a person's eyes. A guilty person will often lick his or her lips. Shame exaggerates the inability to look into a person's eyes. The head bobs down. Guilt and shame are sometimes accompanied by flushing, blushing and perspiration on the person's face.

Disgust-Contempt.   A person who feels contempt usually distorts his or her mouth. One eye may squint slightly as one corner of the upper lip is raised. Disgust signifies rejection or repugnance. Imagine tasting sour milk. Both corners of your upper lip will draw up and your nose will wrinkle.

Interest-Surprise.   Interest is characterized by an upward, wide-eyed expression. The face is relaxed and sometimes the lips part. The eyebrows are lifted slightly. Surprise is rapid and intense interest. The whites show completely above and below the iris. The mouth opens and the person inhales.

Happiness-Joy.   When a person is happy, he or she has an "open" look. The cheeks rise, the nostrils flare and the corners of the mouth pull back. The jaw is relaxed, and the top teeth do not touch the bottom teeth. The eyes communicate as the outside corners crinkle into "crow's feet." The head lifts slightly, changing the light on the eyes and making them sparkle.

Caring-Loving.   The caring-loving continuum is the most difficult emotion to describe. Most people describe a loving look as a "star gaze" or "soft" eyes. Loving is a complex emotion and "the look of love" is probably a cross between interest and happiness. Interest contributes an unblinking stare, whereas happiness contributes a slight smile. This slightly tightens the cheek muscles and gives a softer, more "personal" look than occurs with interest.

What Emotions Do

Although most people do not intentionally use them, emotions serve us in many ways. For instance, distress and anguish usually accompany withdrawal. People who see someone distressed will usually want to help. Anger and rage usually help people get what they want. Anger is one of the most powerful controlling behaviors. Because it is often a prelude to violent unpredictable behavior, people not prepared to counter force with force often withdraw in the face of anger. (No pun intended.) Fear usually leads to and accompanies protection. The body is aroused. Adrenaline is pumped into the blood. The attention is sharpened. People are ready either to defend themselves or to run away.

Guilt and shame show submission and therefore afford protection. When people bow their heads in shame, they simultaneously make themselves vulnerable by not being able to see the other person and by leaving the neck exposed. Disgust and contempt are gestures of rejection or repulsion and signify that people do not want to be close to the objects with which they are displeased. Interest and surprise focus the attention and sharpen the responses. Happiness and joy signify incorporation, an openness to experience. Tension is released and the muscles are relaxed and prepared for stimulation, which explains why public speakers often begin with jokes or funny stories. Caring and loving focus attention on others, yet in so doing the person is also restored and nurtured.

When we see someone express an emotion, we react with some emotion. Our responses are so ingrained that they occupy little conscious attention. This can unintentionally cause communication difficulties. When I was a graduate student, I discovered that my desire to relieve others' pain sometimes hindered their expression of feelings. Since then I have practiced restraining myself, trying to not rush in immediately to relieve distress. To help people make lasting changes we must unite with them to attack the problems that most concern them. Often they must experience strong emotions as part of the battle. Our reactions to those expressed emotions are crucial.

For example, when the person being helped strikes out in anger, the helper might respond with fear, distress or anger. None of these is appropriate. The Bible counsels helpers to be patient (Prov 14:17), to give soft answers (15:1), to avoid quarreling (20:3), to overlook offense (19:11) and to avoid revenge (24:29). We are exhorted to be slow to anger (Prov 14:17, 29; 29:11; Jas 1:19-20) but *not* to withhold anger totally (Ps 4:4; Eph 4:26).

Fear commonly elicits either of two reactions: fear in return or contempt of the fearful person. Our proper response is faith (Ps 23:4; 27:1; 46:1-2; 56:3-4; 118:6; Prov 29:25; Mt 10:26-31), which will produce courage and love (1 Jn 4:16-18).

A person who is guilty and ashamed will usually look down. When the help seeker raises his or her eyes to look at a helper's face after revealing some shameful act or thought, the helper often lowers his or her eyes in shame. The helper is ashamed to view another's shame. If this happens (as it frequently does), the help seeker may become angry. This sequence is quite common in a helping situation: shame-shame-anger. If the person seeking help expresses disgust or contempt, the helper often responds similarly. Interest or surprise by the help seeker will commonly produce caring or loving in the helper. Happiness and joy are frequently shared, as are expressions of loving and caring.

Your training as a helper, however, should not be based on the most common responses of other people. You need to determine *your* most common response to each emotion. To identify how you react to each emotion, have a friend demonstrate each emotion in Table 3. Instead of trying to identify what is happening on his or her face, pay attention to your own emotions. Do you have strong reactions to any emotions? Which ones? What do you feel? What do you want to do when you see each emotion?

As you interpret the emotional messages people send you, be aware of three facts. First, facial expression of emotions changes rapidly, usually every five seconds. (One exception is interest, which can be maintained for up to forty-five minutes.) Because emotions change rapidly, helpers need to watch the faces of help seekers very carefully. During conversation, people usually play peekaboo, intermittently checking for emotional reactions and fixing their glances elsewhere. We concentrate more on what we intend to say next than on what the other person is saying now. Consequently, we try to not look at things which distract our attention from what we are going to say; that is, we ignore the person's face, except when we want feedback about our ideas. On the other hand, in a helping situation, especially during Stage 1 (Understanding), helpers try to encourage people to express and understand their problems and their reactions to the problems. Helpers will therefore seek as much information as possible about the problems, including what emotions surround the problems, before beginning to explore possible solutions.

Second, people may try to hide their emotions from others and from themselves. When we expose our emotions, we become vulnerable. Therefore, most people are skillful at hiding emotions, even if unintentionally, by disguising them in one of three ways. They may *intensify* one emotion, thereby hiding others. One common instance of this is the expression of great distress (crying) to mask anger. In our culture, a woman often cries when she is angry because she feels it is socially inappropriate to express anger, or because she fears that the more powerful person with whom she is angry will strike back. People may *hold back* all emotion, assuming a "poker face." Others *mask* emotions, intentionally replacing an emotion with an entirely unrelated one.

Third, nearly all people forbid themselves to express at least one emotion. Cultural taboos inhibit a man's ability to express distress. When it *is* an appropriate emotion to feel (for example, when his wife dies), he may therefore behave in odd ways.

Handling Strong Emotions

Expect to see people experiencing strong emotions. At times, you may want to change a person's emotional level. Sometimes this is possible by intentionally changing your behavior. For example, Sue is in a crisis. She needs to take action yet she continues to cry, as she has for the past forty-five minutes. You may want to encourage her to stop crying so she can act. On the other hand, Jack has experienced a grievous loss. His father has died. He says that he wants to be able to weep for his father, but he feels no emotion. You recognize that Jack has totally intellectualized his experience since he heard of his father's death. Jack wants you to help him "get in touch with his emotions."

To help someone like Sue stop crying, take careful stock of your motivation by first asking yourself, For whose benefit am I concerned? Is it for mine because *I* am uncomfortable with tears? Or is it truly for the help seeker's? Then ask, How, specifically, will the other person benefit if he or she stops crying?

If you can answer these questions to your satisfaction, then take action to help dry up the rivers of tears. First, ask the person not to cry. Second, direct his or her attention to *thoughts* or *behavior* rather than *feelings*. Third, shift the focus from present or past happenings to plans for the *future*. Fourth, speak as unemotionally as possible. Fifth, as a final measure if the others fail, tell the person to "go ahead and cry for a couple of minutes and get it out of your system." Paradoxically, this has the effect of helping many people stop crying. But it is risky, sometimes making people angry. Thus it should only be used in an emergency.

To help a person like Jack to feel *more* distress, reverse any of the above. Be present-oriented. Focus on feelings. Have the person imaginatively re-enact the distressing event.

Each method of handling distress could be applied to each emotion. Emotional intensity is decreased by asking for a plan and by focusing on thoughts and behaviors. Emotional intensity is increased by focusing on the present or past and by talking about present feelings.

Strong emotions are natural to emotional problems. They can help or hinder a helping relationship. By learning to recognize emotions and your responses, you can be a better helper.

7

Messages That Don't Help (Stage 1)

My goal has been to develop a concept of good communication to help us understand people. One way to do this is to consider both positive and negative examples. For example, a child is taught the meaning of *cow* by showing him or her many cows (positive examples) and then showing that a watermelon is *not* a cow, nor are a dog, a horse or a bull (negative examples). This technique also is used frequently in helping situations. Questions beginning, "What is the difference . . . ?" help sharpen understanding.

In this chapter I will discuss negative examples of communication before I describe how to understand the problems of the help seeker (chapter eight) and how to communicate that understanding (chapter nine). Some communication techniques are not *wrong* (few are in an absolute sense) but merely

mistimed. You try to get your friend to rethink the problem
(Stage 2) before you understand the problem (Stage 1), or
you try to create an action plan to solve the problem (Stage 3)
before you understand the problem (Stage 1), or you suggest
an action plan (Stage 3) before your friend rethinks the problem
(Stage 2). Most ineffective communication results from poor
timing. Other communication techniques are simply ineffective.
We have observed others use them, usually when we were
quite young, and have repeated them without examining their
helpfulness.

Bill corners you at the water fountain. He looks around,
ashamed, then says quietly, "Look, I need some help. My son,
John, is taking an economics class. He's a junior in high school.
Last night my wife went to Parents' Night. That's when parents
follow their child's schedule and talk to his teachers. Well,
Sally came home all in a dither because John's economics
teacher said that he was going to spend three weeks talking
about Marxism. I can't believe it! Sally was so upset. Frankly,
I really don't know what to do either. What do you think?"

What would you say to Bill?

Here are some responses that probably would *not* be very
helpful.

Let Me Ask You This...
1. *"Why does it bother you?"*
2. *"Why do you think that the teacher would teach Marxism?"*
3. *"Why does John want to take economics?"*

There is nothing wrong with asking questions of the person
who is seeking help. In fact, in this example, you certainly would
want to find out much more about the problem before you
suggest any action. The three questions above might be helpful, but they are so specific that your friend may feel inter-
rogated. A police officer questioning a suspect usually has
desired or expected answers in mind. The questioner has a
guess about the cause of the problem, as we discovered in
chapter five. Guesses are not easily laid aside, so we continually

try to confirm them by gathering more information and twisting it to fit.

This pattern of interrogation is often combined with an interpretation, which suggests a new way for the person to view a situation. Typically, the helper gets an idea about the cause of the problem—and therefore about a possible solution—asks a series of questions aimed at supporting the idea. At last, when "sufficient" evidence has been gathered the helper offers the idea to the person. If that insight is rejected, the helper may try to convince the person that the insight is correct, to gather more information to support the insight (punctuated later by a gentle "I told you so"), or to start over with a new guess.

The underlying assumption is that if a person, such as Bill, knows *why* he does something, he will be able to control his behavior. This was one of the early theories of Sigmund Freud, but even he abandoned it.[1] Nonetheless, the assumption has permeated our society. Few, if any, professional counselors today believe that understanding the cause of a problem will alone solve the problem and instead affirm that insights must be put into concrete action before they are useful.

Why doesn't this interrogation-interpretation pattern work? One reason is that it contributes little toward your understanding of the problem from your friend's point of view. Specific questions direct the answerer to where you want to go; in fact, anything you say directs your friend's attention in some way. Because people talk about the things other people will listen to, helpers continually influence the other person. But in Stage 1 you want to influence your friend to talk of the problem from his or her own perspective.

A second reason that the interrogation style is ineffective is that people do not like to be led to someone else's conclusion. This is especially true for people who seek help because most have an idea of what should be done when they ask for help; therefore, early in the helping process, you should listen to the other person's ideas. This not only leads to more mutual respect and cooperation, but it also helps Bill discover soon that his way of understanding the problem is not effective (if indeed it is not) and prepares him to rethink the problem.

A third reason is that many guesses about the cause of behavior are not supported by information from your friend's life. After several false starts in which unsupported lines of questioning are tried, Bill may think that you neither understand nor are capable of understanding.

There, There, Friend
4. *"I wouldn't be so upset if I were you."*
5. *"Don't worry. Things will be okay."*
6. *"Well, I'd be concerned too, if I were you."*

There are times when reassurances and sympathy are appropriate. These times, however, occur much less often than reassurances are given. The times for such support are when all of your cards have been played and when your friend has already been helped. The person needs to know then that you will be there while he or she tries to cope with the situation. Glib reassurances that everything will turn out all right may be interpreted as, "I really don't understand you, but I hope you get better," or "I feel uncomfortable when you express those emotions, so I will reassure you and you will stop making me so uncomfortable." If Bill receives that message, even if you did not intend to send it, communication soon ceases.

You Think You've Got a Problem?
7. *"You think you've got a problem? Let me tell you about my kid's religion teacher at college."*

As a helper you may want to say, "I really identify with you." Perhaps you are eager to share some of your recently acquired wisdom in dealing with a similar situation. You might long to cheer up Bill by comparing his lot to yours. Regardless of your intentions, the you-think-you've-got-a-problem approach produces a predictable response: "This 'helper' doesn't want to understand me, and is too self-centered to ever understand me."

That Old Problem?

8. "Yeah, we had that same problem with Sue."

The assumption underlying this approach is that what worked for you will probably help anyone else who has a similar problem. This assumption is questionable. To communicate efficiently, we label our experiences. If I say, "My son is disobedient," I could mean anything from "he murders people" to "he hesitates for two seconds before doing exactly what I tell him." If I say, "I'm depressed," I could mean that I am a little blue or that I am so clinically depressed that I have not gotten out of bed for three weeks. The flexibility of language is both a powerful tool of a helper and a cause for concern (see chapter ten). If we react to the labels that people apply to their problems, we may try to help in a stereotypical way. Remember that each person is unique and experiences things uniquely. Seek to understand Bill's uniqueness, especially during the first stage of helping. Recall also that the first stage of helping never really ends: we merely add other stages to it.

Let Me Give You Some Good Advice

9. "Why don't you pull John out of that class? He probably doesn't need it to get into college anyway. Besides, it's early in the year."

10. "You ought to go directly to the president of the school board about that."

There is nothing wrong with giving a person direct advice *when* he or she asks for it. In fact, this is one of the things that nonprofessional helpers do best. Most personal problems are resolved long before they become emotional problems because someone gives good advice, the person follows it and the problem is solved. But pick up a textbook on counseling, and the first thing you will see, in capital letters, italicized, with a box around it, is this:

> *NEVER, NEVER GIVE ADVICE.*

Professional helpers see clients for whom advice from many friends has not worked. Clients are, as a result, skeptical of advice. They do not believe that any quick advice will help at all. In fact, they usually don't want to be helped too easily because it might look as if they had been "faking it." Without realizing it, they often resist even the best advice. Most of the people that you will help will not have problems so developed that they are resistant to good advice. I am not recommending that you load up with helping bullets to charge out and machine-gun the world with wisdom. Do not give advice before you are sure that you understand the problem from the point of view of the person needing help. In addition, your chances for success will increase if you patiently wait until the problem has been rethought before you suggest advice.

It is usually too early to give advice if you do not know the following: (a) the person's understanding of the problem; (b) what alternatives the person has already considered and rejected, and the reasons why; (c) what alternatives the person is now considering; and (d) what will happen if each alternative is tried. If you give advice before you know at least this much, then more often than not your advice will be either refuted or ignored. When someone asks you for advice, say to yourself: "Wait! Do I know how this person has been thinking about the problem and what he or she has considered doing about it?" Remember, your friend has probably spent much more time thinking about the problem than you have.

Let Me Tell You about *That*
11. *"Look, there's no problem with just learning about Marxism. John has a strong faith in the American way of life."*

Although all people need to learn a great many things, they seldom like to be taught by a peer unless they ask. To be taught in a condescending way puts people "one down" and makes them argumentative. Have you ever argued heatedly about a topic that you do not actually care about? My guess is that unsolicited lecturing or teaching triggered it.

I'll Take Care of It for You

12. "I know the principal. I'll call him up for you and complain."

If your friend has a need that you are able to meet, your temptation will be to immediately do anything in your power to help solve the problem. At first blush this sounds great. But sometimes helping is *not* doing something.

The "I'll-take-care-of-it" approach might indeed take care of it, but Bill does not learn to help himself. Self-help can be a valid goal.

I'll Bet *I* Know

13. "It sounds as if Sally is suspicious that the economics teacher will expose John to ideas that are different from hers."

Although Sigmund Freud made many important contributions to the field of psychology, one of his techniques is poison in the hands of the untrained. Speculating about Bill and Sally's motives can kill your relationship with them. Even most professionals steer clear of such interpretations. Trained psychoanalysts often conduct at least ten hours of analysis to make one small interpretation of motive.

Interpretations usually provoke hostility and rarely improve a relationship because they say, "I know your inner motives better than you do," which elevates the analyzer above the other person. If the interpretation is accurate, the person analyzed feels exposed—psychologically naked. If the interpretation is inaccurate, then the person analyzed feels misunderstood or even accused.

Psychoanalysts use these interpretations because they accept Freud's theory of how psychological change occurs. Freud claimed that conflict is the essence of life.[2] In particular, he believed that unconscious motives were always at war to control behavior. Because these motives were unconscious, and therefore not available to the person for logical examination, effective helping made the person *aware* of these unconscious motives. Then the person had to learn to *control* them. To discover these unconscious conflicts, Freud had to provoke the person to act them out. This conflict behavior was called the transference neurosis. Once the person's behavior toward the analyst made the conflict apparent, the analyst could interpret the unconscious motives, making the person aware of the motives so that they could be "worked through." If the analyst rushed the interpretation, called "wild analysis" in one paper by Freud, then the person might resist the interpretation.[3] He believed that resistance was not a bad phenomenon; in fact, he thought that progress in therapy depended on it. His method of counseling was designed to create resistance.

For example, he sat behind the patient, who had to lie on a couch and talk of anything that popped into his or her head (free association), regardless of how silly it seemed. These techniques alone make many people hostile and resistant. But Freud had many other tactics. He refused to talk except for very short, infrequent sentences. He always answered a question with a question. He seemed to have all the answers and, most pertinent to our discussion, he speculated about unconscious motives. Many (if not most) therapists prefer to encourage cooperation from their clients. This teamwork approach seems more suited to counseling between friends than does the Freudian resistance-enhancing approaches.

Now Here's Where You're Wrong

14. "Why did Sally get so upset over that?"
15. "What's wrong with learning about Marxism?"

Being judged is a part of growing up. To be young means not knowing as much as the adults in your world. Teachers, parents, neighbors, and even older siblings and peers have corrected, reproved, scolded and chided us. Bill would be a very rare person indeed if he did not react to such judgment and criticism. Emotions demand much attention—attention Bill needs to solve his problem. Criticism can also evoke countercriticism and anger, which slam doors of communication. The most important reason for not judging, however, is that

Jesus said not to (Mt 7:1-5).

Being aware of the pitfalls of poor communication may prevent errors in helping. You still need to know what to do to understand a specific problem. The next chapter suggests what to look for in this first stage of helping and how to get your friend to tell you what is important. It also discusses crucial decisions you will have to make after being asked for help.

8

Understanding Your Friend's Problem (Stage 1)

What kind of attitudes should I cultivate to understand the problem from my friend's point of view? How do I begin to explore the problem? What questions need to be answered early in the helping relationship? What do I look for to help me understand the problem? This chapter seeks to answer these questions. In addition, you'll meet my friend Phil. Over the next five chapters, you will listen in as I counsel Phil, and you will see how this model of helping is put into effect.

Preparing to Understand the Problem
One night my pastor called and asked me to see a woman who was having marital problems. Because she and her husband were new to our church, I had had only one, brief conversation with her. As I rode my bicycle to work the next morning, I began

to pray, asking God about the woman's problem. An unusual thing happened: I had a sense that I knew exactly what was wrong with that couple's relationship. That afternoon she confirmed the knowledge which God had given me. Although God's message for her was not pleasant, she accepted it as accurate. God had supernaturally intervened and used my prayer to provide relief to a troubled marriage.

On another occasion, I was counseling a client. Though my office was arranged with Christian plaques, Christian counseling books and Bibles which clearly proclaimed "a Christian works here," the woman had never mentioned God or anything religious. Suddenly, during the seventh session, I began to pray silently and specifically that God would convince her of her need for him. Within a minute, she stopped in mid-sentence and began to relate her story of falling away from her Catholic faith. She poured out guilt and shame over her behavior, and as I watched, speechless, she repented. That moment of silent prayer—though I never broke eye contact with her and never interrupted her—turned her life around.

Prayer is the most important step as I prepare to interview someone for the first time in a counseling setting. In these two instances God answered in visible ways. On other occasions his answers have been less obvious: God is the author of diversity. He works in many ways. He miraculously, by fiat, created the universe from nothing, and every day he continues to create plants, animals and people by using the natural world that he made. As C. S. Lewis has argued, Jesus turned water into wine in an instant, yet at the same time God was turning water into juice within growing grapes from which wine would later be made, something no less miraculous because it took a little longer.[1] In the same way, praying for friends at times results in rapid healings. At other times, the healings are slower and require the skills of a trained counselor. In any case, God is the healer and our prayers are one vehicle he uses to give us what we do not deserve—grace. I pray expectantly for the instantaneous miracle of healing for the people I counsel, but

I also prepare my mind for the slower miracle of healing through the counseling relationship.

If God has planned a slow healing of the person, then we as helpers need to cultivate several attitudes. These attitudes are helpful in all stages of helping, but they are essential during the early stages, especially the initial contact. First, your task in Stage 1 is not to help the person rethink the problem and not to plan some action. *Your main task is to gather information.* Of course, if a Band-Aid remedy is needed, do not withhold it, but try harder to understand. Second, *wait patiently until you thoroughly understand the problem.* Third, *appear confident and competent.* One of the marks of a truly confident person is the ability to say, "I don't know," when confronted with a baffling situation. Do not be afraid to admit your fears. Realize that even if you cannot help a person solve the problem, you nonetheless offer valuable gifts: listening, sharing the person's struggle, loving and helping the person get help. Fourth, *show warmth, concern, empathy and understanding.* Most people will eagerly talk about their concerns if they believe that you understand and care for them as unique people (see chapter nine). Unfortunately, few people are naturally warm and empathic. These qualities can be learned, but they must be practiced before they feel natural to the helper. This is one reason that psychologists must have at least four years of supervised counseling experience before they receive their doctorates. As you use the good listening skills described in the next chapter you may at first feel awkward, but you will become more and more polished.

In addition to praying and setting my mind on positive helping attitudes, I remind myself of two mistakes that inexperienced helpers sometimes make during early interviews. Sometimes they are too task oriented, and sometimes they are too person oriented.[2] When helpers are overly task oriented, they focus almost entirely on the information that the help seeker gives. They continually sift the information, trying to perceive patterns. They wonder whether their friend has talked in enough detail (or too much detail) about a particular concern. They plot what to talk about next. Lost in this flurry of intellectual activity are the people who are seeking help, people with feelings. Another temptation is to be lured onto the rocks of cold intellectualism by the sirens of interesting emotional problems. On the other hand, when helpers are overly person oriented, they become so wrapped up in the other's feelings and in the way that difficulties are presented that all structure is lost. Rambling, emotional narratives that tell helpers little of the true problem often result. Stage 1 of helping requires a balance between ferreting out information and being sensitive to the person.

Another common Stage 1 mistake is due to our natural tendency to make assumptions. We need to avoid assuming that we know what vague words mean. To do this, listen naively. Ask for explanations of key words that seem unclear. Be concrete. Ask for examples. Get details. Two of your most useful questions will be, "What do you mean?" and "How do you know?" Listen naively and you will guard against incorrect assumptions.

How to Begin

The best way to begin a discussion of a problem is to use an open-ended statement or question—one that cannot easily be answered briefly. The more vague and far reaching the question, the more freedom the person has to tell you what he or she wants.[3] One example of a very broad lead-in is "What would you like to talk about?" Less sweeping is, "Tell me what is bothering you" or "What is the problem as you see it?" An even more restricted beginning might be, "You told me a little about your problem on the phone. What else can you tell me?" Each of these openings asks for description and provides encouragement for the person to talk at length about the problem.

Under some circumstances, you might begin an interview with a different focus. For example, suppose that your friend

Jesse loves to complain at length about all the things that are going wrong in his life. Beginning the discussion with "How can I help you?" focuses Jesse's attention on the particular concerns with which you might help and suggests that you expect to do more than listen to his complaints. Similarly you could ask, "What would you like to change?" This opening says clearly that you expect change.

Although different people react differently to these leads, two patterns of behavior are common. People in pain often "psych up" before seeking help. Emotional problems usually result in much emotionally charged mental rehearsal. A person ruminates on problems as if the instant-replay button on a videotape machine were stuck. It is not surprising then that, when invited to talk, the person will describe his or her plight elaborately and talk eloquently of how it developed. When the story begins, the helper often feels that the floodgates have opened, dumping tons of problems. When this happens, listen carefully, trying not to interrupt. Encourage your friend to tell the story in his or her way. After about thirty minutes most people seem to run out of steam, and information gathering will be more productive for you and less frustrating for the help seeker.

On the other end of the spectrum is the one who assumes that you know the "right" questions to ask and waits patiently for you to begin the questioning. Admit that you do not know what questions to ask. Point out that because the person has thought about the problem much longer than you have, he or she can best describe the problem. Another technique, described by Arnold Lazarus, is called the inner circle.[4] Lazarus sketches five concentric circles labeled A at the center through E on the outside. He explains that these circles represent information about the person: circle A is very personal concerns and circle E is information that is public. For example, circle A might contain sexual concerns or doubts about self-worth. Circle E might be as ordinary as well-liked foods or opinions about the weather. Circles B, C and D have intermediate concerns. Lazarus then tells his client that most emotional problems involve the inner circles and asks, "What level of concern would you be willing to share?" The reluctant person soon begins to talk.

Questions to Be Answered in Stage 1

By the time you have finished the first interview, you should be able to answer four questions. Some you may be able to answer soon after the interview begins, some you will initially answer one way and later change your answer because of new information, and some you will be unable to answer until the interview is nearly over.

1. What does this person want from me? As strange as it may seem, most people do not want merely to get over their problems. They want lots of things from you. They may understand many or only a few of their reasons for seeking you out. Here are several possible reasons why people ask for help (in addition to their main purpose of seeking change).

First, prayer. People often want others to pray with them and for them because Scripture is clear that corporate prayer is powerful. For example, Jesus is present when people are praying together: "For where two or more are gathered in my [Jesus'] name, there am I in the midst of them" (Mt 18:20). Some people want *only* your prayers; most, however, want your help too. Although Christians usually like to be prayed for, some feel uncomfortable *while* being prayed for. When prayer seems appropriate, simply ask, "How do you feel about praying together right now?" If the person wants to pray, simply begin and, at the end of the prayer, pause briefly to give him or her an opportunity to pray. After about ten silent seconds, conclude with "Amen," and resume your conversation. If the person is not comfortable praying aloud with you, then supplement your silent prayers with a short closing prayer. For some you may wish to pray regularly; for example, our family prays daily for members of our own extended family and for three other families we know. We have prayed for some people for over five years and have seen the great effects of persistent prayer.

Second, advice. Many people want to be told what to do. As we discovered in chapter seven, most helpers err by offering solutions before knowing the problems, a natural reaction for people who care about others. Offering quick advice usually makes you feel better for having done something, regardless of whether it helped your friend. Only well-timed advice helps a person in pain, so do not advise too quickly. In addition, offer advice as an alternative rather than as an answer. What works for one person may not work for another. Be enthusiastic and positive in describing what worked for you when you had a similar problem. But your recommendation should nevertheless be tentative: "It worked for me. If you try it, it might work for you."

Third, rewards. People are likely to repeat behavior for which they are rewarded. Rewards are not always as tangible as food for hungry people; some are very subtle social behaviors, such as praise and attention. Whether something is rewarding depends on its context. When adults have such long-standing problems as prolonged depression, marital problems or child-rearing difficulties, they are often rewarded by attention from their friends. "Are you feeling better?" friends ask with concern, and long conversations about how to cope with problems follow. Anyone likes to have others be interested; consequently, attention from friends can reward problem behavior. This does not alleviate the emotional pain. Some may even give up hope of finding any solution. Yet they continue to seek help because of the attention they get. Potential helpers should be aware that some people want attention more than help.

Fourth, commiseration. "Matilda is always complaining. If it isn't her corns, it's her long-lost nephew who's driving her crazy." We all know Matildas who just like to gripe. Often they want agreement that their problems are too difficult to solve. Sometimes they want sympathy. Sometimes they just want to talk. What they want from you is a listening ear.

Fifth, game playing. Eric Berne, in his system of psychology called Transactional Analysis, analyzed habitual communication patterns, which he called games. A game has a beginning, an end, a set of rules, a payoff and three main positions (victim, rescuer and persecutor). There are usually two participants who switch among the three positions. One game, for example, is "Why don't you. . . . Yes, but. . . ." Sarah and Katy are accomplished players. Sarah begins by assuming the victim role, requesting help: "I'm so depressed, Katy. Can you help me?" Katy assumes the rescuer role and offers a series of helpful suggestions which begin, "Why don't you. . . ." To each suggestion Sarah says, "Yes, but . . ." and gives an objection. The patience of Katy the rescuer inevitably wears thin, and she becomes the persecutor. "You don't want help," she snaps. If she is angry, she might yell, "I've tried everything I know, and you're hopeless." Once the rescuer has become persecutor, the victim can feel truly victimized and can self-righteously retort, "You don't care about me. I was just asking for help, and you blew up." Katy, all apologies, will again try to rescue: "I'm sorry. I don't know what came over me. Why don't you. . . ."

With participants who are cooperative, this game can continue for a long time. The payoff for Sarah is a feeling that Katy cannot solve her problems and is therefore "not O.K." This allows Sarah to feel better in her own eyes—"You are one-down, so I am one-up." Katy also gets a payoff, feeling superior because Sarah is unable to solve her own problem. No true help is given or received. Each is working to put the other one-down so that she can feel one-up. Unfortunately, their one-up feelings are accompanied by negative feelings such as frustration for the helper and, in this case, depression for the victim.

Helpers should avoid becoming rescuers. There are a number of ways to avoid a game or to free yourself from a game; for example, begin by asking what your friend wants to do about his or her problem. By not offering to provide *the* solution, you may prevent a game from getting underway. If you have made several suggestions which are not acceptable to the help seeker, say, "I've given you a number of suggestions, and I'm really baffled about what would help. Do you have any ideas?" Or you might say, "Can we write down a few of these suggestions? Even though they don't seem helpful to you now, they might after you have prayed about them." A determined game player is tough to handle. Your best bet is to not get involved in a game in the first place.

Lastly, support. Many people want to be with others during times of stress even though they do not want advice. Perhaps they want to face their problems alone. Perhaps they already know how to solve their problems. They are seeking reassurance that their friends and families support them. In such cases, do not give advice; it will not be appreciated.

Because people do not generally want only one response from helpers, you must guard against a simplistic approach to problems. If you assume that a person wants only advice or other concrete help (and not support, prayer, attention, the chance to complain to a willing listener, or even the chance to engage you in a game) you may behave simplistically and not fulfill the expectations you and your friend hold.

2. Can I help or not?   One of the most difficult things for friends to learn is when to say no. A dangerous assumption that many helpers make is that love and understanding conquer all. They think that because they have good intentions, they can help anyone who has a problem. They cannot. Even highly trained and experienced psychotherapists occasionally work with clients who actually get worse while in therapy; less highly trained and experienced therapists have even more such clients.[5] This is especially true when a person's problems are severe. Without question, psychotherapy helps many people solve their problems better than no psychotherapy, yet a few people get worse.

When people decide to enter therapy, they usually do so because they have been unable to solve their problems with the assistance of family, friends, physicians, employers, teachers and pastors. For many, their hope is nearly gone, eroded by the tears caused by advice that has not helped. Each bit of help offered by a friend raises the hope of the person with the problem. Each failure makes success that much more difficult. This does not mean that friends should not try to help. For each 100 people who come to therapy, 33 to 45 could conquer their problems without the help of a professional therapist—many by the help of their friends. With the help of both therapist *and* friends, 67 to 80 would conquer their problems.[6]

Consider carefully the kind of help you can offer. Think especially about your competence in dealing with the person's particular problem, your time and energy, and the resources of the other person. To evaluate your competence, you must be able to estimate the severity of the other person's problem (this chapter will help you). You must also consider your past experience with similar problems. No two problems are exactly alike, so new skills will develop with each person that you help. Sometimes, however, the chasm between your experience and the person's problem is bridgeable only with the most unstable rope ladders. In these cases, do not risk raising the person's hopes that you will be able to help. Listen and try to understand the person's problems (Stage 1) but admit that you cannot offer much beyond that. Then offer to refer the person to someone more qualified to help. You might also offer your continued support (Stage 4) and interest (Stage 5), depending on the time and energy you are willing to commit to the person.

Even Jesus could not help everyone. Many who heard his message did not heed it (Mt 19:16-22; Mk 6:5-6). Others simply never heard because, as a finite person while on earth, Jesus did not have the time, energy or resources to reach everyone. Jesus gave some people a great deal of time and attention: John was his favorite (Jn 13:23; 21:20); Peter and James were also his intimates (Mt 17:1). The other disciples received much of his care, but his acquaintances received less. Some people felt his healing touch briefly. Others passed him in the street, perhaps without knowing it. Realizing he could not do everything, Jesus carefully managed his time to accomplish God's will. We, too, should try to be good managers of the time and energy that God has given us. When God brings needy people across our paths, we should consider what type and amount of help we are to give. A timely referral to a person competent to deal with a particular problem can be more loving than hours of ineffectual conversation. Yet this does not excuse us from helping those we are qualified and called to help. Like the expensive ointment that Mary poured over Jesus' feet, our lives give off a sweet fragrance when they are poured out in the service of Jesus.

Professional help is often expensive, even though many agencies and private practitioners now use sliding pay scales, and insurance sometimes pays for psychological counseling. The financial strain of expensive therapy can increase the pressure of an already troublesome situation. You need to consider the alternatives to professional help that your friend has. Many pastors are excellent counselors. Some are not. Some church support groups are quite therapeutic. Many elders are fine counselors. A wide circle of friends or a supportive family might also come to your friend's aid. Rarely are you the only avenue of help. Consider the entire social network of the person. Remember that trying to help when you are not competent can damage your friend, regardless of your good intentions.

3. Should I refer this person to a professional?

Sometimes the best step you can take is to secure the opinion of a professional before continuing to help. Six guidelines can show you when to recommend professional intervention. First, when the person endangers himself or someone else, recommend help. If a person threatens suicide, regardless of how serious *you* consider the threat, the person is "at risk." Second, when a person feels that he or she is losing control over behavior, thoughts or emotions, and when you cannot help the person regain control by your conversations, recommend help. Third, when a person requests professional help, honor that request. In general, the person is the best judge of whether professional help is needed. Fourth, when a problem seems extremely troublesome, recommend a professional consultation. Fifth, if a problem bothers a person for a long time or is quite severe for a shorter time, encourage the person to get a professional opinion. Sixth, if the problems seem to get progressively more serious, recommend professional help. Mehrabian and Reed have summarized these by suggesting that problem severity depends on three factors: distress, uncontrollability and frequency.[7]

If any of the guidelines above are applicable, ask the person directly whether professional help is needed. If the person thinks not, do not be afraid to admit that you feel inadequate. You might say something like, "Karen, the way you describe what's happening with you is sort of scary for me. I really have not had much experience with these problems. But professionals deal with them daily. Maybe a short time talking with a counselor would save you a lot of time spent feeling upset the way you do. Of course, you are the best judge of what you need, but consider it. I'm glad to give you all the love and support I can, but that may not be enough to get you through these troubles very rapidly." When in doubt, suggest a professional consultation rather than risk harm to the person. Seeking a professional's opinion about a problem does not commit your friend to future contacts, but it will give an objective assessment from someone who does it routinely. Many professions include counseling in their job descriptions. Clergymen, for example, have often taken courses in counseling during their training for the ministry, though their supervised experience is usually limited. A pastor who is not qualified to counsel can refer people to a professional counselor.

Professional psychological help is available from schools, university counseling centers, community mental health agencies, private counseling agencies, hospitals, state mental health institutions, and psychologists and psychiatrists in private practice. Of course, the military and some large industrial firms have their own professional counselors. The professionals who work in these various settings are from different academic backgrounds and include social workers, counselors, psychologists and psychiatrists. A social worker usually has a master's degree in psychiatric social work and is trained to provide individual and group therapy under the supervision of a psychiatrist or psychologist. A counselor usually has at least a master's degree in counseling and can provide individual and group counseling in schools, rehabilitation centers and agencies.

A psychologist usually holds a Ph.D. in either counseling psychology or clinical psychology and works not only in settings similar to counselors but also in hospitals and in private practice. Psychologists usually must be licensed by the state in which they practice, which certifies that they have passed a state licensing procedure designed to protect potential clients. Psychologists who are not licensed are supervised by a licensed psychologist. Psychiatrists are physicians who have completed a residency (usually at least three years) in psychiatry. They alone of all providers of psychological services may prescribe drugs. They work in private practice, in hospitals, and in state-supported mental health agencies. One referral source for emergency consultations is the emergency room of a hospital or mental health center. Most hospitals, especially those with psychiatric wards, maintain a psychiatrist on duty (or on call) for emergency psychiatric assessments. In a crisis, a person may walk into an emergency room and request help.

If you get a reputation as an effective helper, inevitably you will talk with people whom you are not competent to help. For such situations, establish a list of referral sources. You can certainly refer to the Yellow Pages' listings for psychologists, psychiatrists, psychotherapists, counselors or marriage counselors, but a recommendation is more effective if you are familiar with the approach of the professional. Consult the Yellow Pages only in emergencies.

Should you refer the person to a professional in an explicitly Christian setting, or is a person in a secular setting equally acceptable? To answer this question, many quote Psalm 1:1: "Blessed is the man who walks not in the counsel of the wicked. . . ." They see this as explicit guidance from the Bible to avoid the secular counselor (understanding that Christian counselors can still function in a secular setting). I believe that such an interpretation is not justified by the context. In light of the entire psalm, I believe that the verse says that the Lord does not favor (bless) those who act in an ungodly way. The intent of the verse is to admonish us to act righteously, as God would have us act, rather than to advise us about psychological counseling. Nonetheless, research has shown that in successful counseling clients' values become more similar to the values of the counselor than they were at the beginning of counseling.[8] Values that affect a person's Christian beliefs are not necessarily those transformed, yet it is important to be wary of the professional's values. Most people seek professional counseling during times of emotional upheaval, when they are vulnerable. Sometimes Christian professionals are not available. Therefore a person who seeks help from one who is not a Christian should exercise caution.

4. What is this person's view of the problem? The crux of a Stage 1 interview is discovering how the person views the problem. Many sources of data are available, but probably the best source is what the person says. Some counselors, especially those heavily influenced by Freud, believe that the person's view of the problem has little significance. Freud believed that the *real* cause of a person's problem was conflict among unconscious motives; therefore, if a person could discuss the cause then, by definition—because the cause must be conscious to talk about it—this was not the *real* cause.

I differ with Freud. I believe that people behave as they do because they have learned to behave that way. They may be conscious of their motives at the time that they act, or they may simply respond by habit. God has given language so we can control our own behavior. Very often our thoughts and expectations, which might be in the form of words or vague images, govern our behavior. Sometimes we act first and think later, but usually we behave thoughtfully. I urge you, therefore, to pay close attention to what people say about their problems. Think long and hard before you disbelieve an explanation. Disbelief often indicates that you are forcing your friend to describe the problem as you see it rather than trying to understand the problem from the other's point of view.

Another source of data is the behavior of the person while talking with you. Pay careful attention to how the person (a) presents himself or herself, (b) solves problems, (c) acts in interpersonal relationships and (d) talks about the problem. By careful observation you can determine how the person answers questions and reacts to stress, whether the person becomes defensive easily, whether the person intellectualizes experiences, how the person deals with strong emotions, and even how well the person is able to understand and use what you say. Get an overall impression of the person's self-concept, confidence and faith. Knowing his or her style of self-presentation will help you put other information into perspective.

Most people develop characteristic styles of solving problems.[9] Some attack problems directly; others ponder solutions; still others react emotionally. Some act impulsively and make the best of the consequences, but others plan carefully and systematically. Some people ask directly for help; others become helpless and lure others to their aid. Still others command people to help them. Some will not accept a solution that does not require action, yet others will not accept a solution that does. If you are able to determine the person's preferred problem-solving styles, you can save valuable time during Stage 3 (Planning for Change). You might even discover that inappropriate tactics are part of the person's problem.

Some psychologists believe that all emotional problems result from faulty interpersonal relationships.[10] Clearly, when a person has a problem, others in the person's social environments are affected. These people may prolong or alleviate the problem by how they react. Consequently, to the extent that the person behaves the same with you as with other important people in his or her life, you may be able to tell how the person elicits reactions from others. Does the person meet your suggestions with arguments? Does the person seem overly dependent? Does the person try to please you regardless of the cost to himself or herself? Answers to such questions can show you how to suggest changes.

Because of Freud's influence, most believe that when people have problems, they are due to underlying *real* problems. They view counseling as akin to solving a mystery in which the therapist, like a detective, alertly identifies clues until at last the real problem comes to light. And, as in a mystery, bringing the solution to light is considered the end of the problem.

This book is built on a different notion. I believe that the same problem can be described in many different ways, from many different points of view. Each perspective yields different actions that the person may take to alleviate his or her distress. Each perspective is "correct" insofar as it describes what is actually happening in the life of the person seeking help, yet some perspectives yield effective solutions and some do not. When a person has a long-standing emotional problem, he or she probably is not viewing the problem from a useful perspective because that perspective has not helped solve the problem. Thus, the helper first must discover how the help seeker views the problem. Later, the helper can suggest new ways.

Suppose that you are having dinner with Lynn and Norm.[11] Talk turns to children, and Lynn says, "Our eleven-year-old son just does not obey us at all." That is one way to describe the problem. It says that the son does not obey and that effective help will concentrate on getting him to obey. But his mother could just as accurately have said, "I really don't know how to get our son to obey me." That sheds a new light on the problem, implying that she has a problem and that effective help will concentrate on her. She also might have said, "Norm and I have been unable to agree on how to discipline our son, so he doesn't obey us." That would have focused on the marital relationship. Yet another way she could have talked about the problem is: "My son and I are at an impasse. We can't agree on what he will do, so I feel like he never obeys me." Thus the mother-child relationship would become the focus of attention.

The way people view their problems are the doorways into their lives. They see their needs in specific ways. Sometimes they think that fulfillment will come when the specific need is met. Jesus recognized this and always entered people's lives through the doorways they opened to him. He healed blindness, a flow of blood, madness and lameness *before* he viewed the person's need from a different perspective—spiritual poverty. The open door is the need as the person perceives it.

In addition to what the person says and what the person does, another source of data about the problem involves contradictions between actions and words or between emotions and words. Differences in these channels of communication reveal uncertainties and mixed feelings. These discrepancies often point to important areas of conflict and vulnerability.

Your gut-level, emotional reaction to a person often serves as a barometer of the emotional pressure felt by others when they are with your friend.[12] For example, suppose that you frequently feel angry after you offer a suggestion to a friend. Ask yourself why. Perhaps the person does something that provokes you to anger, such as dismissing your suggestions as unimportant or not responding in any way. Perhaps the anger stems from your own lack of confidence. If you are able to identify something the other person is doing that provokes your angry feelings, then you must decide whether you will say anything to the person about it. Your guiding principle should be: Does this help the other person reach his or her goals? If you can see a clear connection, share your reactions with the person; if not, keep the reactions to yourself. The tendency when you experience negative reactions will be to share them and thereby "benevolently" punish the person.

Resist this. Sharing your own reactions with another person can be devastating.

When Phil Asked for Help

We have discussed how to begin an interview and have equipped ourselves with tools to enhance it. Let's meet Phil.

The phone rang a second time before I reached for it. "Hello," I said. Silence... then the hint of a sob. "Hello," I repeated. More silence. "Who is this, please?"

"I don't know," a voice said huskily.

But I recognized that it was Phil, a college student who attended our church. "Is this Phil?" I asked.

A soft grunt, vaguely affirmative, was the only answer.

"Phil, you sound upset. What's wrong?"

"I need to talk. Do you have some time?"

"Sure. Come on over. Do you know where my office is?"

"Yeah. It'll take me about thirty minutes to get down there. Is that okay?"

"Of course. Would you like to tell me what's bothering you?"

"I'll tell you when I get there. See you in about thirty minutes. Bye."

Phil was on his way to my office, a young man with a problem. He was obviously quite emotional, which alerted me to be sensitive to what he communicated through his emotions. He had always seemed shy during church functions, and I wondered how easily I could get him to talk about what was bothering him. If our phone conversation was any indication, he would not be verbal. My immediate tasks were to understand the problem from Phil's point of view, and to decide how much help he needed and from whom. How was I to proceed?

My interactions with Phil demonstrate the main stages of helping. Throughout chapters eight through twelve we will follow the progress of our counseling sessions. Phil is a composite, representing several people who have had similar concerns, concerns that are fairly common among high-school and college-aged people.

Phil: Session 1

Phil arrived about forty-five minutes after he called and knocked hesitantly at the door.

1-Me Come in.

1-Phil Hi, Ev.

2-Me Did you have any trouble finding the office? Oh, have a seat.

2-Phil Thanks. No, no trouble. Look, I'm not bothering you, am I? I mean, if I am, I can come back some other time.

3-Me No, this is fine. I have the next, let's see, fifty minutes free, then I have a meeting that I have to go to. [I paused. Phil did not respond for about ten seconds.] You sounded pretty upset on the phone.

3-Phil Yeah, I feel kinda dumb now.

4-Me Dumb?

4-Phil You know, like a little stupid for getting all worked up over nothing.

5-Me You probably thought a lot about it as you drove here.

5-Phil Uh huh. I almost didn't come in. Waited around for about ten minutes trying to decide. Since I'd told you I would come, I thought at least I could drop by and talk a while. [Phil gave a short, forced laugh but the corner of his mouth quivered.]

6-Me Do you want to tell me what it was that got you upset? It might seem silly now, but it probably was pretty important to you then.

6-Phil Yeah, it was. [He paused, a half smile frozen on his face, but his eyes were moist and a tear leaked down one cheek.]

7-Me [Obviously, Phil was still very emotional about whatever had upset him. He seemed ashamed to cry, yet the intensity of his emotion was preventing him from talking freely about his problem. As long as he fought the tears, he would be unable to tell me.] Phil, I sense that whatever happened really upset you. In fact, it is still upsetting you. It sounds like you're a little embarrassed about it and about talking about it. Is that one of the reasons that you had trouble deciding whether to come on into my office?

7-Phil Yeah. [He lowered his head, ashamed. Tears crawled onto his shirt.]

8-Me [After a minute or two.] Phil, there's some tissue right beside you on that shelf. I know that it's embarrassing for you to be so upset. It probably doesn't help for you to know this, but it doesn't bother me that you are upset.

8-Phil [He nodded.] I'll be okay in a minute. [I waited. After blowing his nose and wiping his eyes, he looked up and smiled tentatively, a real smile for once.] Yeah, I guess you've seen all this before.

9-Me Well, I've seen a lot of people very upset, but it seems that each person has a different thing that upsets them.

9-Phil Well, I feel better now.

10-Me Good. Do you want to tell me what got you so stirred up?

10-Phil Well, really, I've had this problem for a couple of months. It's bothered me a lot. [He paused.] Oh, it's really too embarrassing to talk about.

11-Me Maybe I can help you get started. Over the phone you said something that surprised me a little. When I asked who was calling, you said, "Nobody," or something like that.

11-Phil Yeah. That's it. I probably said, "I don't know who's calling," 'cuz that's what's been running around in my head all these weeks—I don't know who I am.

12-Me What do you mean exactly, that you don't know who you are?

12-Phil Just that. I seem to be so many different people, and I don't know which one is the real me.

13-Me So you act very differently at different times and that makes you confused and upset about your identity?

13-Phil Right. I don't know my identity. That's what got me so upset today—identity. You see, I was reading this novel that a friend said was real good. It's about this guy who loses his identity and spends the whole book trying to find out who he is. Everybody's betraying him and trying to kill him and he only has one person who will believe in him and that's this girl. It devastated me!

14-Me You really identified with him in some important ways, and that scared you.

14-Phil It sure did. Of course, I don't pretend to be a spy, like that guy, or anything like that, but I kept seeing myself in his problems. The more I read, the more I thought that I must be schizophrenic or something—you know, one of those multiple personalities. I read about them this semester in my personality class.

15-Me So you thought that you must have some pretty severe problems, and that upset you. [He nodded.] I can see how that would really bother you.

15-Phil Yeah.

16-Me What makes you think that you might have more than one personality?

16-Phil Just that I feel so different in different situations. I mean, I don't act like a schizophrenic or nothing.

17-Me What do you mean by "act like a schizophrenic"?

17-Phil You know, having amnesia. Doing crazy things and then kind of coming to and finding myself somewhere and not knowing how I got there. That kind of thing.

18-Me And you say that you *don't* do any of that kind of thing.

18-Phil No.

19-Me So it's just "feeling different in different situations" that makes you think that something is wrong? [He nodded.] Can you give me an example of when you felt like that?

19-Phil Okay, let's see. [He paused.] Well, yesterday at church, for one. I felt very good and real close to God. That was a real good service we had. [I nodded.] But just the night before I was out with some guys, and we went to this bar even though I really didn't want to. Now, I don't drink very much, but we got to talking about some girls and trading rounds of beers, and I guess I got a little high. Can't you see? It's like I was two different people. I don't feel like a hypocrite, because I really love the Lord. But nobody's perfect. It's not like it was a little sin in an ordinarily spotless life. It's like I was two people, two totally different people, either all one way or all the other.

20-Me You seem really confused by it all. You say that you know you did wrong but that that's okay because nobody's perfect. You imply that it is a little sin, then turn right around and say it is a giant sin. It's almost like you are wrestling with yourself, struggling back and forth. First one side of you gets on top, then the other. And you can't tell which side is going to win.

20-Phil That's it exactly! That's why I feel like two people. I'm tearing myself apart.

21-Me As if two wrestlers are tugging and pulling on part of you and, if one wins, you'll explode.

21-Phil Except, now that I think of it, it's not just *two* wrestlers. It's lots of wrestlers, all pulling in different directions.

What Is Phil's View of the Problem?

Though my conversation with Phil did not end here, let's take stock of what we know about him. We have only a general view of the problem: Phil is confused about the many roles he plays. I have listened to him describe the problem and have tried to show him that I understand his confusion, his shame, his distress. I have tried to show that I understand the content of what he says by rephrasing his conception of the problem into a metaphor that is new to him (the wrestlers). I have listened naively, getting him to explain what he meant by the words *schizophrenic* and *multiple personalities,* not assuming that he and I understood the words to mean the same things. In light of the goals of the first interview, I have made some preliminary decisions. Phil seems truly to want to change his situation. He brands himself with emotion-laden words such as *dumb, schizophrenic* and *multiple personality.* My guess is that he seeks reassurance that he is not "crazy." He also seems distressed enough to agree to a number of counseling sessions for relief. I have cursorily tested whether dealing with Phil's concern falls within my area of competence. Based on the information that Phil has given me thus far, his problem seems like a normal developmental problem faced by many young people, even though he is reacting more strongly than most young people. He might later add concerns that change this evaluation, but at this point no referral is warranted.

I know one thing that I would not ordinarily know so early in a first interview. I can answer the question, "What brought the person for help *today* rather than yesterday or perhaps last week?" Phil's problem became a crisis as he read a novel about a man with similar concerns. When a crisis precipitates help seeking, the person usually will be more motivated to change than if he or she merely "decided" to talk to you today.

At this point in the interview, I need to clarify many details about the problem as Phil understands it:

1. How severe is the problem? How often is Phil greatly distressed by his confusion over his identity? What is his usual emotional reaction? Is today's reaction typical?

2. How long has the problem existed? Exactly how did it begin? Have there been ups and downs?

3. Specifically, what usually happens right before and right after the problem occurs? Examine several specific occurrences.

4. What things make the problem worse? better?

5. What differences are there between times when the problem bothers him and times when it does not?

If Phil has wrestled with his problem for two months, then he has probably tried several ways to cope with it. To help him think of *new* ways to cope, I must know what he has already tried. As Phil tells me about his solutions, I will ask him why those attempts have failed. If he does not understand clearly that his solutions have been ineffective, then he will not be receptive to other solutions. Finally, two more bits of information are necessary: what Phil thinks could be done to solve his problem and what kinds of social support he has to help him change. Let's continue our first session.

Understanding Phil Better

22-Me So you feel as if many wrestlers are pulling you in many different directions.

22-Phil Yeah.

23-Me That sounds very confusing for you.

23-Phil You can say that again!

24-Me You mentioned the conflict you felt over getting high on Saturday and then going to church the next day and having a good experience worshiping the Lord. What was another time you felt this wrestling match?

24-Phil Well, every time I think about school.

25-Me What about school?

25-Phil Well, I can't decide whether I should stay in or drop out.

26-Me So you kind of argue with yourself. . . .

26-Phil Uh huh. My parents—especially Dad—would be really mad if they knew that I was even considering dropping out. Then I think that I don't like it very much. . . .

27-Me Don't like what?

27-Phil . . . don't like school very much. Except for a couple of courses. I liked my psychology courses—some of them. But I could never major in psychology because there are so many courses that I don't like that I would have to take if I majored in it. But I don't have the slightest idea what I would do if I dropped out of school. I guess I could go to work for the department store where I work part-time now. But then that's business, and I'm majoring in business now, and I don't like it. You see? I just fight with myself over this and get nowhere.

28-Me It's kind of like in *Fiddler on the Roof.* Did you see that? The. . . .

28-Phil Yeah. The old guy kept going, "On the other hand, such and such, but on the other hand . . ." back and forth. But at least he decided. I just keep going back and forth.

29-Me And that discourages you.

29-Phil Yeah, and scares me a little too. I mean, I don't think it's *normal.*

30-Me You're worried about having some psychological problems?

30-Phil Uh huh. Is it normal?

31-Me Well, from what I have heard you say so far, it sounds as if you're having some difficulties that are fairly common among college students. But just because a problem is common doesn't make it any less painful.

31-Phil Don't I know it! But it's good to hear that other people have problems like this. Look, there's one other problem that I spend a lot of time wrestling with. [Phil gave a nervous laugh.] I guess it's pretty common these days. I guess this is probably the thing that kind of triggered all my worries about myself. I wasn't going to tell you about this, but I guess it'll be okay.

32-Me I think it would help to know how this all got started.

32-Phil Well, about two months ago, I went to a movie with Karen. [I knew Karen and Phil had been dating for over a year. Both attended our church, but Karen was more involved in church activities than Phil was.] The movie wasn't very good, I suppose, and it had a lot of sex and stuff in it. [Blushes.] Well, after the movie we went back to the apartment. I knew that both my roommates didn't usually come home on Saturday nights. You can see how bad this was. Well, uh, one thing led to another and . . . well, I tried to take off, uh, Karen's. . . . Well, anyway, she wasn't having any of *that*. But I just kept on trying. Finally, she got angry and kinda yelled at me to stop. We had a long talk about sex and things, and she said that she was going to be a virgin on her wedding night, no two ways about it. But one thing she said during that talk I just haven't been able to get out of my mind. And it's so simple too. I ought to be able to forget it. She said, "You really scared me. You're like a totally different person when it comes to sex." After she said that, I just kept thinking about it over and over. I realized how right she was. In so many areas I'm just all these different people, and I don't know which one I really am. Boy, I never thought I'd be able to tell anyone *that!*

33-Me Let me see if I have all this now. About two months ago, Karen said that you were like a different person when it came to sex. Since that time you have thought, periodically, that you might really *be* different people. One part of you wanted to have intercourse with Karen, but one part didn't.

One part of you wants to drop out of school, but one part doesn't. One part of you wants to live a life pleasing to God, but one part doesn't. Is that right?

33-Phil Well, you put some of those things a little more strongly than I would have, but I guess that is the general idea.

34-Me What things did I put too strongly?

34-Phil Well, I truly want to live a life that's pleasing to God, but I *can't*. It's not that I don't want to. It's like I don't have any control over what I do sometimes.

35-Me You think that something prevents you from acting the way that you would like?

35-Phil It's not really that. It's like . . . things just happen and I go along.

36-Me How about the other things—were those accurate?

36-Phil [He paused at length.] Yeah. At first, I didn't think you were right about there being part of me that didn't want to have sex with Karen.

37-Me But now . . . ?

37-Phil Well, now, I realize that there is a part of me that wanted Karen to stop me. That's hard to admit to myself, 'cuz if you don't want to make love, maybe there's something wrong. And I don't want to even *think* about that.

38-Me You're saying that if you decide not to make love for some reason, even though you do have normal urges to make love, then there might be something wrong?

38-Phil That's a better way to think about it. It really doesn't mean that something is wrong with me. It just doesn't tell me whether or not I *can* make love. Yeah. [He paused, thoughtful. After a minute, he looked up at me.]

39-Me Look, Phil, I'm going to have to go in about ten minutes. Let me ask you a couple of questions before we say good-by for today.

39-Phil Okay.

40-Me I need to know some things about what happens when you get upset over these thoughts of the many Phils. For instance, how often do you get upset?

40-Phil All the time.

41-Me You mean every waking hour?

41-Phil No, but at least once a day.

42-Me Does anything in particular get you thinking about it?

42-Phil Well, I think about it a lot at night, after the light is out and before I fall asleep. Sometimes I have a hard time getting to sleep because my mind is racing. Also, anytime I see my roommates, especially when they are with their girlfriends, I get to thinking about what Karen said. I guess those are the two main times I get upset over it. Oh, yeah, every time I go to my econ class. Gee, I hate that class!

43-Me At those times you get pretty upset?

43-Phil Well, in different ways. Econ makes me mad. I just think about how much I hate school but can't do anything about it.

44-Me And when you see your friends. . . .

44-Phil Then I think that they must think something is wrong with me because they're all sleeping together, but I'm not.

45-Me So you worry about what your friends might think of you, and that makes you doubt your own adequacy. And it also makes you think that you don't know the real you?

45-Phil Exactly.

46-Me And at night . . . ?

46-Phil That's the worst. I think about all of those things, and especially how I might be crazy or a split personality or something.

47-Me So nighttimes are the worst. How about this one today? How did it compare?

47-Phil This was the worst ever. But it was kind of a freak in a way. I mean, how many books will I read about somebody losing his identity? No more. I'll tell you that!

48-Me Let's see. Can you summarize briefly what you got out of our talk today?

48-Phil Well, for one thing, I never in a million years thought I'd tell you all that I did. Just telling it to someone who will listen is a big relief. It's funny, but now that I think about it, I feel much

124

better than I have in months. I don't feel like I'm crazy, even though I still feel very confused about who I am. I feel like I understand myself a lot better than I did, and I know more what the problem is.

49-Me And what's that?

49-Phil Well, confusion over school and sex and living a Christian life. Do you think I'll be able to get over the confusion?

50-Me I think you can probably clear up some of the confusion if you are willing to work at it.

50-Phil I am. I'm tired of this struggle all the time.

51-Me Then how about if we get together and talk next Monday at this same time?

51-Phil Sounds great! You're sure you have time?

52-Me Sure. Oh, one thing you might give some thought to this week is how you cope with this worry about your identity once you start worrying.

52-Phil I'll do it.

53-Me See you next week.

53-Phil Good-by.

Evaluating the Interview

Considering the time strictures, this interview with Phil was fairly successful. As often happens, Phil brought up many of the questions that needed to be answered without my having to ask. Notably, he volunteered information about the event which triggered his help seeking and the event which began the problem. As also often happens, some questions remained unanswered or not answered in sufficient depth. Subsequent interviews can fill in the details, especially specific identification of the difference between times when the problem is strongest and times when the problem does not bother him, and ways in which he has tried to cope with the problem.

The object of the interview was to understand Phil's problem from his perspective. In general, I did this and communicated that understanding to him. One weak point in the interview occurred when I summarized the three critical issues Phil had talked about (33-Me), and he objected that they were worded too strongly (33-Phil). That was a bold confrontation for Phil, who often seems influenced by what others say—Karen, his father, his roommates and now his counselor. (In fact, this overdependence on others might be one of the things on which Phil needs to work.) Phil communicated that he strongly believed that he could not control his actions at times, that "things just happen and I go along" (35-Phil). Future interviews will explore the different ways Phil views his problem.

The helping process with Phil is well under way. In chapter nine we will examine the tools of this process, communication techniques that allow helpers to express their understanding to others.

9

Showing You Understand (Stage 1)

If you understand people completely, yet cannot or do not let them know that, you will do little to help them. Any solution that you propose will be rejected. The people may even feel that talking to you is a waste of time. In some ways, communicating your understanding is the essence of helping. In fact, Carl Rogers, one of the most influential psychologists of the last four decades, for many years emphasized active listening as the *only* thing needed for effective psychotherapy. Many training programs for paraprofessional helpers concentrate almost exclusively on active listening skills.

As powerfully therapeutic as they are, active listening techniques are impotent if separated from the content of a problem. Consequently, I have described what information to look for (chapter eight) before I described the tools to discover the information. Why are these tools so important? What are they, and how are they used?

Why the Emphasis?

Anguish comes from feeling trapped, alone with pain. When I have an emotional problem, I am isolated with my pain. I focus my attention on my problem, which erects towering walls around my mind. I struggle to escape but time after time my pain banishes me to my shell of aloneness. Active listening cuts holes in these prison walls. I know that someone out there cares.

Christians know that Jesus cares for us and will set us free from whatever walls bind us (1 Pet 5:7; Gal 5:1). When we pray, Jesus listens (Mal 3:16; Ps 6:9). But not only does he listen—what good would a giant cosmic ear do?—he also acts.[1] Yet even while knowing these truths, Christians can have problems when they turn their eyes on their pain rather than on Jesus. Our active listening can remind people of Jesus' presence and his care. It can remind people of Jesus' love as they see his love in us. Jesus is the healer, and by showing that we understand and by being identified as a Christian, we can point people toward him.

In addition to defeating loneliness, communicating our understanding of a problem can help a person form a more accurate understanding of his or her problem. By freeing the help seeker from the trap of endless ruminations, the helper can identify sources of confusion and uncertainty and can embolden the distraught to face inadequacies. By promoting self-understanding, the helper can mobilize one of the greatest resources for solving problems—the help seeker's own ideas. People who have problems are more involved, invest more energy and have more direct knowledge of the problem than helpers ever can. Usually, however, they are stuck, unable to break out of old ways of thinking. When someone really listens, such a person can often conceptualize the problem differently and can thus help solve it.

A third benefit of communicating our understanding to people is the release of emotional tension. Problems usually seem more manageable when they are discussed. Because we struggle to organize our experiences when we talk about them, we can feel more in control simply by putting our problems into words. Moreover, we can blow off steam—perhaps even overreacting in the presence of a sympathetic person— so we will not overreact in the face of a difficult situation.

Communicating Attitudes
In 1957 Carl Rogers suggested that change took place in psychotherapy because helpers were able to create a climate characterized by certain attitudes.[2] He, and others after him, showed that these attitudes did not appear magically but that helpers act systematically to create and preserve such a climate.[3] As you practice the skills described in this chapter, remember that they should create a therapeutic climate in which the person feels understood. There is no one correct way to establish such a climate; different people act differently and achieve the same results. Some are warm and kind. Others are strong and forceful. Still others are aloof and intellectual. Despite personality differences, six attitudes will make it easier for others to believe that you understand them. Three focus on the help seeker (respect, empathy and acceptance); three focus on the helper (openness, genuineness and concreteness).

People deserve our respect. God has created them valuable. If people were not valuable, Jesus would not have died for them. (And he died for them even when they were not Christians.) Because God values all people, so should we. Respect prohibits us from remaking them in our image, forcing our decisions on them when we think that "it is for their own good." God gave people free choices that we must not take away. We want the people we care about to triumph over their pain when they are hurting, but they may choose not to change. We need to show our respect by listening to them, not judging them, and working to understand them. We need to reward people for their achievements, rejoicing with them when they rejoice (Rom 12:15).

Empathy means experiencing another person's world as if you were that person, suspending your own ways of feeling and understanding, desiring wholeheartedly to see things through the other's eyes. To measure your empathy, frequently ask your friend how well you seem to understand what is said. Empathy is not merely a summary of content. It includes understanding emotions and hidden meaning. True empathy is rare and takes a great deal of energy, but it pays big dividends.

One of the most difficult attitudes for many Christians to maintain is acceptance. Because God told people things in the Scriptures that are true, Christians often treat as worthless a person who does not agree with that truth. We know that Jesus told us to love even our enemies (Lk 6:27). We know that he exhorted us not to condemn a person regardless of his or her sins (Jn 8:2-11). Yet we have a hard time practicing our beliefs. Perhaps that is why we are commanded often throughout Scripture to refrain from judging. When we accept a person we might disagree entirely with his or her beliefs. We might even believe that the person's actions are self-destructive. But we continue to value our friend and his or her right to consider the behavior to be reasonable, even when we disapprove.

Openness is listening willingly to descriptions of problems that are personally threatening to us. It is easy to become anxious and defensive and try to steer the conversation to other topics. Some helpers feel nervous when talk turns to homosexuality, divorce, temptation, sexual inadequacy or even overeating. If we become anxious at the mention of a topic and prevent help seekers from discussing it, other doors of communication may close. This is not a blanket admonition to listen to everything that another person wants to discuss. There are times when you should decline to hear a problem. For example, a single male probably would feel very uncomfortable listening alone to a woman discuss the sexual problems she has with her estranged husband. In such a situation, state straightforwardly, "I feel that I wouldn't be very much help to you on this matter. I'm sure that someone else could give you more help."

Though we temporarily suspend our biases as we listen empathically, we continue to be ourselves, to be genuine. This means we reach spontaneously toward others without being totally uninhibited. It also means sharing ourselves when that helps. Genuineness is simultaneously being real, being sensitive to the other person and being aware that we should concentrate on our friend.

The vaguer the problem, the larger it seems. A nebulous problem cannot be solved, but a specific problem could be. Helpers must develop a tenacious desire to have problems described specifically. For example, Bob says, "You can't tell what's going to happen when you mess up. Somebody might jump on you." You could say, "You seem uncertain about some things." But a more concrete response would be, "You seem afraid that your boss will criticize you if you don't repair that machine perfectly." Bob states the problem vaguely by using the pronoun *you* instead of *I,* and by using *somebody* instead of *my boss.* He also does not clarify what *mess up* and *jump on* mean. The first response, although capturing part of Bob's feeling, leaves the problem statement unclear and menacing. The second response, on the other hand, encourages Bob to talk more concretely by translating the generic *you* into "Bob," *somebody* into "Bob's boss," *mess up* into "not repairing that machine perfectly," and *jump on* into "criticize." The second response also labels Bob's unstated feeling as fear. These translations and labels might not be wholly accurate from Bob's perspective, but at least they force him to elaborate by correcting those that are inaccurate. As a result, the problem will be better described after Bob and the helper reach an agreement about it. Commitment to the attitude that talk should be specific will result in more intense, more helpful and more interesting discussions—both while you are helping someone and while you are talking casually with anyone.

Active Listening Skills

Active listening skills are basic and are applied throughout the helping process. Other tools are more advanced and usually should be used after the first stage of helping, with a definite objective in mind. I will discuss and illustrate each skill individually, beginning with the basics.

Counselors in training typically spend one week practicing each skill before tackling the next. This might include participating in a workshop which describes and illustrates the skill, and provides opportunities for role plays that use the skill. The counselor then might role play (and videotape) other situations during the week, viewing and criticizing his or her own videotapes as well as those of others in training. The counselor will also practice the skill, when appropriate, during normal conversations that week. At least one semester is spent practicing these skills; it often takes years, however, before these techniques feel natural. Be realistic, therefore, about your abilities. Merely reading summaries of skills will not make you an excellent helper. Becoming a good helper takes years of practice. But, reading these summaries should sensitize you to the many types of listening tools at your disposal. I hope, too, that you will practice these skills at every opportunity.

As you read, you will realize that you have used almost every one during normal conversation. Yet most people habitually use only a few, though they are able to use all of them. Hone your gift for helping: practice continually. When you are in a helping relationship, consciously use some of the skills that you do not ordinarily use. This will expand your working repertoire of skills and increase your flexibility, making you a more effective helper.

Attending.   Attending is serious business. It is hard work. It is listening *plus,* which communicates active involvement. It is the cornerstone of a helping (or any other) relationship. You attend to people *to understand* them, *to show respect* and *to keep the topic focused* on one or two specific concerns. All three are vital to effective helping.

How do you attend effectively? First, maintain eye contact. Eye contact suggests that you are listening to what the other person is saying and makes you appear trustworthy. It should be fairly constant but should not be a steady stare. Occasional breaks are necessary, but frequent breaks are usually interpreted as inattention. Identify the times you break eye contact—they probably occur when you are threatened, embarrassed or concentrating on your own thoughts. Notice when the other person breaks eye contact and you will learn what is embarrassing, threatening or thought-provoking to him or her.

Second, become fluent in body language. To communicate involvement, squarely face the other person (whether you are standing or sitting), and adopt a relaxed and open position, leaning slightly from the waist toward the person, arms and legs uncrossed. Use gestures to communicate high energy. After long stretches of conversation, you can boost the energy level of the conversation if you make a visible shift in posture. The best time to do this is during a natural break in the conversation. For example, suppose Sharon has just finished telling you about her problem with overeating. You have listened attentively. She says, "Well, that's it. What do you think I ought to do?" You two had been sitting with your heads about thirty inches apart, and you were leaning forward from the waist at about a ten-degree angle. After her question, pull your chair about three inches closer and lean a little farther forward to about a twenty-degree angle. This will put your heads only about five inches closer then they were, but your actions communicate, "Okay, let's get down to work on this. We can lick it!" Try this little shift sometime during a conversation with a friend and see what an astounding effect it produces.

Third, use verbal following. This means to become intensely interested in what the other person has to say. If you can do this, avoid interrupting the person or jumping from topic to topic, and avoid talking about yourself or your experiences, then verbal following will take care of itself.

Following responses. Following responses encourage people to keep talking. Sometimes they are called "minimal encourages." Nodding the head, a short "Uh huh" and a longer "Hmmm" each show that you are listening and following the person's line of thought. Other short following responses are:

I see.	Oh?	So?
I understand.	Interesting.	Then?
Is that right?	You don't say.	Tell me more.
How about that!	No fooling!	And?
Really?	You did, huh?	Did you?

Of course, these responses are not equally appropriate for all situations. Don't use them mechanically. Be sensitive to the situation and genuinely interested in the person, and convey this through your following responses.

Restatement. Repeating what the person has said can clarify meanings by allowing the help seeker to hear his or her vague language. A short repetition demands more specific information. If an irate husband says, "I'm sick of the way she always gets her way," the helper could respond, "She always gets her way" or simply "Always." Exaggerations and distortions are shown for what they are, which encourages a more accurate picture of the situation. Restatement is a good way to request more information while staying on the topic that your friend introduced. It interrupts only briefly and focuses attention on specifics. Restatements can be considered a type of following response.

Silence. In normal conversation when one person stops talking, regardless of how briefly, another person begins to talk. Consequently, we feel uncomfortable and tense when silence sets in. We try to relieve tension as quickly as possible by asking a question, offering reassurance or even proposing a solution. Instead, consider periods of silence from the help seeker's point of view. They often are less aware of the silence than helpers are. People in emotional turmoil who have just talked about their experiences may be trying to make sense out of what they said. What seems like an unbearable silence to you may go by very quickly for a person who is upset and needs time to ponder the implications of what was said. A well-timed silence that allows your friend to think is a positive communication, indicating that you respect the help seeker and his or her ability to think through a problem.

Do not overuse silence, though. People expect you to respond after they relate their problems. Also, use silence more during the initial outpouring of the problem than during subsequent conversations. Avoid the needless confrontation that results when silence becomes a test of wills. Finally, if a person indicates that he or she does not know what to say, do not use silence. Return to a previous topic in which the person has shown interest.

Focusing.   As an active listener you can greatly influence what the other person will talk about. Carl Rogers, the founder of "nondirective" or "client-centered" counseling, believes that feelings are the key to a person's values. Therefore, he often comments on his clients' feelings and his clients, not surprisingly, talk about their feelings. Albert Ellis, a psychologist who founded a therapy that emphasizes rational reasoning, pays attention to his clients' thoughts—and so do his clients. In the same way, you too will guide your friends in their talking, whether or not you are aware of doing so.

Your response to a statement will in turn focus a person's response to you. Ivey and Gluckstern maintain that you can respond to a simple statement by focusing on one of six topics.[4] Suppose that Anne has marital difficulties. She says, "I just don't know what to do. It's so miserable living with Gene. Every night we seem to find something to argue about. I know that he doesn't like it any better than I do, but we're trapped."

First, you could focus on her thoughts and feelings by saying, "*You* feel cornered, like there's no way out. That must be frustrating and painful for *you*." Anne's attention would be directed inward.

Second, your answer could focus on yourself: "Anne, *I've*

felt trapped and cornered in *my* job at times. It has seemed as if all *my* choices were painful. Are your feelings something like *mine*?" This helps Anne know that you have felt some of the same things that she has felt, which splits her attention between her feelings and yours.

Third, your reply could center on someone else: "As you say, *Gene* probably doesn't like the pain any better than you do. *He,* too, must feel frustrated and reluctant to go home each night." This would encourage Anne to see the problem from Gene's point of view.

Fourth, a response could focus on your relationship with her: "Anne, I'm really glad that you have told me all of this. I feel *we* have a common bond. I think that *we* can really do something about this painful situation if *we* work at it *together*." This directs Anne's attention to the idea that teamwork can be an asset for her and it openly acknowledges the closeness of your relationship.

Fifth, you could concentrate on the topic: "Real *arguing* is never much fun when *it* involves someone that we love. *Arguing* splits apart relationships." Such a response is more impersonal and encourages Anne to talk intellectually about what she should do. If Anne were highly emotional, you might choose this focus to reduce her emotion.

Finally, you could emphasize the social aspects of Anne's experience: "I know what a bind you must feel. Each day you work at your church and see *a lot of people* who highly value traditional family life. But perhaps there are a few people *in your 'world'* whom you can openly talk to." This response would help Anne think about those who would support her during her time of trouble.

We have enormous power to direct conversations by even the shortest responses. On the other hand, almost every statement above had more than one emphasis, giving your friend choices of how to respond. This can lead to frustrated helpers who try to help others focus their attention and are thwarted at every turn by those who are determined to avoid an area.

Remember that relationships depend on both people. Do not assume too much or too little of the responsibility for helping someone else change.

Questions.   If not overused, a question is one of the best ways to get a person talking about his or her problems. Questions can elicit general information, put a person at ease by encouraging conversation, request specific examples that illustrate the help seeker's problems or solicit specific information you need to understand the problem. One of the most important functions, however, is that they focus the person's attention where you want it focused. How can you use questions effectively? Here are five guidelines to point the way.

1. Don't play "Twenty Questions."   Conversations can turn into question-and-answer sessions: you ask a question, the help seeker answers but then waits, which pressures you to ask another question. This pattern develops because you have either used closed-ended rather than open-ended questions or you have been testing your guesses too early. Closed-ended questions invite a short response, often a single word, and begin, for example, "do you," "will you," "can you" or "who." They imply that you know exactly what you are looking for, and they allow you to direct the conversation where you want. They are useful when you lack specific bits of information. On the other hand, open-ended questions elicit longer answers and begin "what," "how," "could," "can" and, rarely, "why." Questions beginning "where" and "when" usually elicit answers of medium length. If you test your guesses too early, you will lead the help seeker to believe that you know exactly what is wrong and will soon provide *the* answer. If you get caught in the "Twenty Questions" pattern, break out of it by asking open-ended questions.

2. Solicit only one answer at a time.   Sometimes helpers ask questions that seek two or more bits of information ("What happened when your depression began, and how long ago was that?"). Two-pronged questions can confuse the help seeker. Usually, one question will be answered and the other ignored.

3. Avoid forced-choice questions. Forced-choice questions allow only a limited number of answers. An example is, "When you became depressed, did you get overactive or did you have inactive periods?" These questions make the help seeker want to shout, "None of the above!" (or "All of the above!"). A variation is a statement followed by "Don't you agree?" or "Isn't that right?" Imagine how you would feel if someone said, "All parents should spank their children when their children disobey. Right?" Regardless of our beliefs on a subject, forced-choice questions put us on the defensive.

4. Use "why" questions sparingly. When I disobeyed as a child, my dad always asked me why. When he did, I felt that whatever the reason I gave for my misbehavior, my dad was thinking, "There is no good reason." Perhaps it is a holdover from my childhood, but when I am asked a "why" question, even today, I feel put down and become defensive. Many people react similarly, perhaps because this technique is a favorite of many parents.

5. Think before you ask. Questions disturb the normal flow of conversation. Before you interrupt to request more information, ask yourself if the information is crucial to your understanding of the person (and his or her problem). In asking for clarification you overtly direct the course of the conversation. While drawing out information that *you* desire, you might divert your friend from volunteering information that is more important. Don't become overconcerned with gathering the facts.

Reflection of content. Paraphrasing, or reflection of content, is not the same as repeating a message word for word. The helper distills a statement and then tells the help seeker what was understood. If used mechanically, reflection is a sterile technique. (During reflection of content drills, counselors in training and their "helpees" have come perilously close to hurting themselves while nodding off and falling from their chairs.) Appropriate and sensitive use of reflection of content, however, can make a conversation smoother, show that you are actively involved and help the person clarify his or her thoughts—all important objectives of the initial outpouring of an emotional story. When a person describes a series of events leading to an emotional crisis, the story is often complex, poorly connected and somewhat incoherent. To be sure that you understand what is being said, occasionally paraphrase the content of the story. This verifies your understanding of the story, conveys your interest, encourages the person to continue talking and increases your trustworthiness. (It implies that you are nonjudgmental.) When you accurately reflect content, a side benefit is likely: you like each other better. This mutual warmth and caring prepares the way for suggestions to be heard and acted on later.

Reflection of content is similar to restatement; both focus on certain aspects of what is said. Restatement merely repeats words, but reflection of content gives the essence of the thought in a compact form which uses words other than those used by the help seeker. Suppose that Marvin says, "I'm really burned out with all this work. I've had to work every night this week. It's exhausting." The helper could reply, "Exhausting" or "Burned out" as a restatement, or "You've really slaved away this week" as a reflection of content.

Reflection of feeling.   To reflect feeling you must recognize and label a person's emotion. Even more than reflection of content, reflection of feeling will strengthen a warm and trusting relationship. You demonstrate that you can appreciate how the person subjectively experiences his or her world, supplementing your understanding of what the person thinks about it. Reflection of feeling also can help the person become aware of, accept and explore feelings. Many people in distress experience several simultaneous emotions which must be sorted out. Reflecting all emotions requires subtle discriminations and could best be done piecemeal—identify one emotion with each reflection, then, after all the emotions have been identified, summarize the mixed nature of the emotions. Sometimes people have trouble talking about their concerns. They begin to tell about their troubles and become stuck. A timely reflection of feeling such as, "It seems as if you have run into a roadblock," or "That's really difficult to talk about, isn't it?" can help the person resume.

Emotions can be hard to identify in a way that accurately captures the experience of a person (see chapter six). Carkhuff and his associates have suggested five steps to effective reflection of feeling.[5] First, observe behavior, paying special attention to facial expressions, voice tone and overall energy level. Second, listen carefully to what the person says. Third, ask yourself, "If I did this and said this, how might I feel?" In labeling your own feelings consider both the category of feeling (such as anger-rage) and its intensity (such as dismayed, frustrated, annoyed, seething, mad, outraged or furious). Fourth, make certain that the person will understand the word you choose; for example, though it may capture the emotion exactly, you would probably say to only a few people, "You feel disconsolate," if they were sad or gloomy. Fifth, put the feeling word into a sentence with a form such as "You feel _____." Note that merely beginning a sentence with "You feel" does not guarantee that you have reflected the person's feelings. For instance, "You feel like your boss is not going to offer you a raise this year" is a reflection of content rather than of feeling.

Summarization.   Similar to reflection of content and feeling, summarization is done after long dialog rather than after relatively short messages. For example, during a story that takes twenty minutes to tell, you might reflect content ten times and reflect feelings fifteen times but summarize only once, at the end or at an important point in the story. Try to capture the essense of a person's experience, selecting crucial dimensions to restate as accurately as possible.

Egan suggests that a summary is helpful on four different occasions: (a) at the beginning of a new session after being apart for several days, (b) when a person seems to have finished talking about a topic, (c) when a self-exploratory process seems to be going nowhere and you want to direct attention and foster coherence and (d) when introducing an action plan (see chapter eleven). He also suggests that the helper occasionally ask the help seeker to summarize.[6]

Putting It Together

Each active listening skill—attending, following responses, restatement, silence, questions, reflection of content, reflection of feeling and summarization—helps you convey your understanding and also provides numerous opportunities for you to verify whether you understand the person. After a reflection of content or a reflection of feeling about which you are unsure, and after most summarizations, check your response by asking your friend whether it is accurate.

The following conversation illustrates these active listening responses. I have identified each response in the right-hand column. Test your skill at identifying responses by covering the right-hand column with a piece of paper. As you read, think of how you would respond as the helper, then look at the helper's response and try to identify what it is. The situation? You have not seen your friend Alan for over a week. You notice him, sitting alone.

You Hey, Alan, how's it going?   *Question (open-ended)*

Alan Okay, considering.

You Considering what?   *Following response*

Alan Well, I feel a little like Job, except I have no ashes to sit in.

You You seem really down. What   *Reflection of feeling*
happened?   *Question (open-ended)*

Alan What happened? I have more problems than I ever thought possible.

You [Silence]   *Silence (hard to fool you on that one)*

Alan You know I was trying to get into medical school?

You Yeah?   *Following response*

Alan Well, I got my rejection notice
yesterday. I guess the world will just
have to get by without my great
healing hand caressing it.

You I'll bet that's really disappoint-   *Reflection of feeling*
ing for you.

Alan Yeah, it is. I'd really counted
on that for a long time.

You It's hard to give up a goal you   *Reflection of content*
have worked hard for.

Alan You can say that again. I put
so much time and effort in it that it
makes me sick. It's getting so I can't
depend on anything I try hard at.

You How so?   *Question (open-ended)*

Alan Mary just dumped me this
morning too.

You Dumped?   *Restatement*

Alan Yeah. Broke off our engage-
ment. After two years! How could
she do that?

You Wow! It's hard to take two re-   *Reflection of feeling and*
jections like that back to back.   *content*

Alan It sure is. Sometimes I don't
think I can take it. Why, if I weren't
a Christian I would be considering
suicide right now. I feel really rejected. God must be punishing me.
Unless things change soon, life
seems like it's not worth living.

You Alan, you sound really de-   *Reflection of feeling*
pressed, as if a great weight were on
your shoulders. You also sound a
little confused. You seem angry at
God and maybe you want to get

back at him, perhaps by doing some harm to yourself. Is that off base?   *Reflection of feeling*

Alan No, that's just how I feel. I *am* angry. I know it's wrong to be angry with God but... but it just does no good to be angry with medical school—or even with Mary. I just feel so helpless. I want to fight the world. I want to hurt everyone, including God.

You And also including yourself?   *Question (closed-ended)*

Alan Yeah, I know I shouldn't, but, well... if there was only something I could do that was constructive.

You What do you think you could do that might be constructive?   *Question (open-ended)*

Alan Nothing—it's hopeless.

You It sounds as if you feel totally powerless, unable even to budge that weight from your shoulders.   *Reflection of content*

Alan Not really, I guess. It's just my bitterness coming through.

You Uh huh.   *Following response*

Alan I guess I could pray for Mary.

You Uh huh.   *Following response*

Alan And I guess I could go back and talk with her. I got so angry when she said she wanted to be able to date other people that I stormed out without really finding out what she was thinking. [Pauses]

You [Silence]   *Silence*

Alan As far as med school goes, I guess God doesn't want me there.

You Yet you know God has a job   *Reflection of content*
picked out especially for you.

Alan Right. It's just that now I have
to find it. And it's such a big world
to look in.

You What is your first step?   *Question (open-ended)*

Alan Well, at the library they probably have some books about health
professions besides being a doctor.
I suppose I could look up a book
like that.

You Are you going to do that?   *Question (closed-ended)*

Alan [Pauses] Yeah, it's a start anyway.

You It sounds as if you were upset   *Summarization*
and discouraged over these rejec-
tions—to the point of despair. But
now it looks as if you've thought of
some options for tackling the prob-
lem. How are you feeling right now?   *Question (open-ended)*

Alan Better. It helps to talk about it.

Add to Your Repertoire

Active listening skills do the bulk of the work in Stage 1, but
sometimes more advanced skills are necessary. Three are immediacy, confrontation and self-disclosure. When timed appropriately, these skills are more powerful than active listening
skills but consequently are more risky. Give careful attention
to how you use them and to their effects.

Immediacy.   The skill of immediacy is focusing on what
happens at the moment that it happens in a discussion. You
may focus on your own thoughts or feelings ("I'm really confused by your last comment"), or on the behavior, thoughts
or feelings of the other person ("That seems to really touch
you—you look like you're about to cry"), or on the relationship
("We seem to be going around in circles today"). It is an important helping skill because almost every emotional problem
affects more than one person. Problems develop and subside

within relationships: you as a helper need to give attention to your relationship with the other person. The way in which you two resolve your tensions and discomforts will help your friend with other relationships.

If you notice that your relationship has soured, initiate an immediacy talk at once. Keep in mind, though, that you need not share all your thoughts and feelings; you must balance openness and sensitivity, and you must consider what will actually help the person reach his or her goals. Be tentative as you share your thoughts and feelings. For example, instead of the accusatory ("You seem to be dependent on me to make your decisions"), I prefer to be more low-keyed ("I feel pressured to make a decision right now. I wonder why I feel that way?"). Do not overdo immediacy. When a person talks about difficult concerns, avoid immediacy. As your relationship develops, introduce immediacy when it is appropriate. Too much, too soon, can threaten a person with intimacy, which closes doors to further communication.

You can use immediacy whenever relationship concerns spring up, but several issues usually result in immediacy talk. One of the most common is in matters of mutual trust. Others are due to differences in lifestyles, values or problem-solving strategies. Immediacy can also relieve tensions in your relationship, channel wandering conversation and resolve the issue of dependency versus autonomy. When you have identified that an immediacy response is appropriate, make it immediately. The longer that you wait after an incident, the less positive will be the effect of your comment. Maintain eye contact and stay relaxed. Commenting on your relationship can be threatening, but fight the urge to look down or away, or to tense as you start your comment. Be relevant to the topic: do not be afraid, even if the topic is threatening.

Because immediacy usually involves what is *not* being said rather than what is being said, continually ask yourself what you are feeling about the other person and why. Be sensitive to your feelings and to the other person's nonverbal communications. Try to frame your immediacy responses in the present tense because you are trying to capture what is happening in the relationship *now*. "You seem really anxious and afraid right now" is better than "You seemed really anxious and afraid." Use "I" language rather than "you" language. (This will communicate that you accept responsibility for your perceptions and do not blame your friend.) A help seeker is likely to become defensive if you say, "You make me angry" or "You are always arguing with me." On the other hand, "I feel angry when you do that" or "It seems to me that we are always arguing" convey the same information but are labeled as your perceptions rather than as fact. Finally, when you make an immediacy response, be ready to follow it up. This is a time for honest, two-way emotional expression. Try not to be defensive. Keep in mind that your objective is to understand the other person and not to win a battle.

Confrontation. When we think of confrontations, we usually visualize head-to-head battles, arguments or even shouting matches. In effective helping, however, confrontation has a much more restricted meaning: accurately pointing out observable inconsistencies. As such, it is not mere disagreement with someone who holds an opinion different from yours. Neither is it a hostile challenge. Rather, it concerns contradictory behaviors. Judgment and opinion should be purged from helpful confrontation. One type of confrontation points out inconsistencies in the help seeker's words or behavior. A helper would say, "You say that you are not angry, but you continually clench your fist and grind your teeth," or "You say you want to stop drinking, but you stop at a bar on the way home from work every day." The other type highlights differences in perception between you and the help seeker: "You say that you're too weak to solve your own problems, but I believe that you have a lot of strength that you're just not using right now."

The purpose of confrontation is not to triumph over or punish the other person. The purpose is to help identify, explore and resolve contradictions thus contributing to a more accurate and consistent self-image. Ask yourself, What are my motives? Are they to help or to be right; to encourage or to get revenge? What specific, observable behaviors are discrepant? Can the person act upon this confrontation? Is our relationship strong enough and intimate enough to withstand the confrontation? State the discrepant behaviors in a way that will promote exploration by the other person. Be tentative. Be prepared to encounter uncertainty and even hostility, and to discuss these and other feelings nondefensively.

Self-disclosure. Normal conversation often includes a series of personal anecdotes. These stories are usually only loosely connected and frequently begin, "That reminds me of the time when Uncle Clarence and I stole an outhouse. You see, we were. . . ." This type of "war story" is *not* what I mean by self-disclosure. Helping relationships are more focused than normal conversation; consequently, self-disclosure within helping relationships is telling other people about yourself as it applies to their concerns.

In Stage 1, telling others about yourself can build a trusting relationship. Your own self-disclosure shows that it is appropriate to reveal personal information, which encourages your friend to reveal personal information to you. Information about your feelings is probably more intimate and should be disclosed after you have revealed less threatening information. During Stage 1, a general rule is that the more immediate your disclosure, the more effective it will be. For example, if you disclose something in the past tense you could say, "I understand how you feel. Several years ago when my widget-polishing business failed, I was really low. I didn't feel like I could face another day." An effective wording would be to continue in the present tense: "Even now when I think about my utter despair, I get choked up."

During Stage 3 (making an action plan), helpers usually talk more about their own past experiences than in other stages to provide an effective model. Among nonprofessional helpers, this is the most used (and abused) form of self-disclosure. Common pitfalls include not qualifying the experience as "my experience" and not carefully relating the self-disclosure to specific goals for change. A good example of self-disclosure which introduces an action plan would be, "Your fear of heights seems similar to mine in some ways. Several years ago I was absolutely petrified of being anyplace I might fall. For the last year or so I've been trying something that has really worked for me. Of course, it may not work for you, but what I do is. . . ."

Before talking about yourself, you must understand the other person. Without understanding, you will be unable to demonstrate the relevance of what you are sharing—and to listen, the person must understand why your experiences are pertinent. When you tell about your experience, use "I" language and "own" your experiences. State the connection between your experiences and those of your friend. Finally, check whether you have been understood. As you talk, watch for nonverbal signs that he or she is not interested or does not understand. At the conclusion of your statement, you might ask your friend to paraphrase how your experiences apply to him or her, or whether your experience sounds similar.

Self-disclosure is controversial. Some professional counselors encourage it, some do not. I believe that when it is used appropriately it can be quite potent. Yet with it come a few cautions. Infrequent self-disclosure makes you seem cool and aloof; if it is too frequent, it can diffuse the focus of your helping. Allow for individual differences, noting, for instance, that some people have little patience when you talk about yourself. As is true for immediacy and confrontation, this skill is powerful. Overuse or very clumsy use can damage a friendship because with greater power comes greater risk.

10
Rethinking the Problem (Stage 2)

Imagine that you are walking through a dark cave. The walls drip with slime. You rub against it, shiver . . . and stumble on. Small, strange sounds creep out of the blackness ahead and steal into your ears. Darkness surrounds you, crushing the breath from you. What lies ahead? Perhaps it is a cliff, and you will step out into nothingness and tumble head over heels into eternity. Or worse, maybe it is the never-ending gloom. Suddenly, ahead, is a person who offers help. A match is struck. You can see where you are. Relief! But where are you going now? How are you to get out of this cave? You have a lit match, but where is the torch that will return color to your world and illumine your goal? Where is that light?

Struggling with an emotional problem is like groping through the gloom. Understanding is the spark which ignites helping.

Yet though your understanding (Stage 1) provides light in the darkness, it does not illumine the goal. Whatever your friend has tried, has failed. The way he or she has thought about the problem has not helped. You need to help the person think in a new way, which brings us to Stage 2 of the helping process. Using the relationship you have developed, you help the person view the problem in a way that provides an escape. But how?

Basically, you will discuss the problem while trying to think of different ways to understand it. As you use the fruits of your thoughts and the results of the focused discussion, you will help your friend focus systematically on the new understanding, finding support for it in the person's life and revising it where support is not found. Gradually, you will introduce new ideas that support the new understanding. You will, at last, summarize what you've done and help develop specific goals. Stage 2 is exciting. You and your friend work closely together to develop a conceptualization of the problem that will lead to clear goals and a powerful action plan. The care, patience and persistence that characterize your commitment differentiates this help from simple advice. It powerfully affects whether your help is heeded.

At the beginning of Stage 2, you have two main tasks which are vital to keep your helping on course. They occur at the same time and there is continual feedback from one to the other. You must *encourage a focused discussion of the general problem* while you *suggest ways to view the problem that the person has not tried.* This approach is built on the assumption that all problems can be viewed productively from many different points of view, virtually all of which can be supported with evidence from the help seeker's life. Some viewpoints produce unique results; some produce the same results as others, but more efficiently. The new perspective depends on your thinking and on the topics that the two of you discuss.

Identifying Problems and Goals
As you think about new ways to view a problem, focus the

discussion on the problem. One good way to do this is to ask about difficulties and goals.

You Paula, let's try to figure out some goals for you. First, tell me what you think your main problem is.

Paula I'm depressed. . . .

Paula responds typically to the helper's inquiry: she labels her problem. Labels may refer to feeling states, personality traits ("I'm not self-controlled"), general problem areas ("I have family problems"), or even psychiatry ("I'm an obsessive-compulsive"). Whatever the labels, they are almost always vague. Your task is to help your friend sharpen the description of the problem.

Paula [Continuing] . . . because Seth constantly nags me. I always get depressed when I'm nagged. My parents used to nag me all the time and get me depressed, even when I was in grade school.

In addition to using a label, which is inherently unclear, Paula has refused to take personal responsibility for her problem by blaming both her husband and her parents. In this way, she implies that Seth has a problem (and should change) and her parents had problems (which caused this whole mess, so they are to blame). But Paula thinks, "I don't have a problem —except with Seth. Good grief! What *can* I do about a husband who nags?" You must help her develop clear, personalized and solvable problem statements. You must find exactly what happens when she becomes depressed.

You So you think Seth *makes* you depressed by his nagging and that your parents are ultimately at fault. Unfortunately, there's nothing you can do about your past, and you can't do very much about Seth's nagging. But you *can* do something about your depression. Tell me exactly how you behave when you get depressed.

Paula Well, I cry and. . . .

You About how often do you cry?

Paula At least once a day, sometimes more.

You Okay, so you cry at least once a day.

Paula And I have a terribly low energy level. I just feel like I don't want to do anything or go anywhere. It's almost too much effort to get up and watch TV.

You So you hardly ever do anything except watch TV. [She nods.] How much TV do you think you watch?

Paula I don't know [sighs]. Pretty much all day, I guess.

More questioning along this line will lead to a very specific statement of the problem which details, as closely as possible, exactly how much of each behavior Paula does during her depression. Such a carefully defined problem can be used to set workable goals. It is not easy, however, because people are not used to describing their problems so specifically. They work hard to develop efficient labels for their problems in order to be easily understood by their friends and acquaintances. These labels, though they aid social conversation, inhibit effective helping.

Problem statements also are rarely clear-cut. People are complex and so are their problems. For example, usually a person is not merely depressed but is also anxious, behind at work and withdrawn from friends. You must help the person list the problems by priority, thereby relieving the feeling that all problems must be solved immediately. The person will then feel more in control. Crises demand attention. If you do not help the person handle crises right away, he or she will probably not pay much attention to anything you say.

Ideally, consider only one problem at a time. Though this is rarely possible in practice, try to help the person keep the number of problems being worked on to a minimum. Therapists usually begin by trying to introduce a small but significant change, which builds momentum and provides the client a successful experience with therapy. This fosters confidence that larger changes are possible. Adopt a similar strategy. Help the person set a small problem as a high priority and try to work systematically toward bigger problems.

One roadblock to this is that occasionally a person becomes

bothered about a problem though you cannot see what relevance it has to the person's overall goals. The person returns the conversation to this problem over and over. You must deal with the problem in some way before progress can be made. Give that problem high priority or assure the person that the problem will be considered later. Regardless of the disposition, you must be considerate of the other's feelings.

In general, take care of crisis problems immediately. Then systematically deal with other problems, beginning with small problems that, if changed, will improve the person's outlook and emotions.

Having done this, you are ready to turn problems into specific goals. Paula, for example, said that she cries at least once a day. You need to find out what she considers to be an acceptable amount of crying.

You Paula, you said that you usually cry at least once a day. By this time next month, how much would you like to have reduced this?

Paula Well, I don't want to cry at all—at least not the kind of crying I've been doing.

You Right, that's sure the ideal. But you've been depressed for quite a long time. And you are right in the middle of a very bad situation at work that doesn't show any sign of changing—not to mention that it might take a while for Seth to completely stop nagging. So it might be a little unrealistic to think that everything will be absolutely happy within a month. What would a good reasonable goal be? To reduce your crying to about . . . ?

Paula . . . to about two times a week.

You Good. If you can do that, it'll make a lot of difference in how you feel most of the time.

Ideally, you should help the person define all goals in similar detail before you consider how to change any one goal (the exception being when the person is in a crisis). This can be tedious, so you will probably specify only the most important four or five goals in such detail, returning to the others as the person works on the priorities. You act as a guide in helping the person set goals. He or she makes the decisions while you insure that all options are considered. Table 4 gives examples of lead-ins to help you focus the person's attention. Considering goal setting only at the beginning of Stage 2 is somewhat misleading because we help people set goals in all stages except the first. Goals are continually set, met or revised, and as helping progresses, the goals become increasingly more specific. This is especially true after you begin suggesting that the person take action.

Goals are an important but almost totally neglected part of most helping efforts. Goals get people thinking about changing rather than about their problems and their negative emotions; in particular, goals stimulate thought about small changes rather than "instant cures." This change of focus from global problems to specific goals concentrates the person's attention and makes lasting change more likely and disappointment less likely. Goals also promote action and help people notice that they have made progress. For you as a helper, setting goals provides time to think and to understand people's problems in new ways.

Rethinking a problem is a creative process. That means it is hard to teach. Yet there are some things that you can do to help. You can cultivate, fertilize and plant seeds of ideas, but only God can make the solutions bloom and grow. To prepare for new ideas, pray for knowledge and wisdom, and trust God for an answer (1 Cor 12:4-11; Jas 1:5). Then ask yourself some questions. Carefully consider how the person views his or her own problems. Do the different problems relate to each other? If so, how? What kind of overall themes keep appearing—in terms of both topics and ways that the person tries to handle the problems? To get a fresh perspective on the person's problem, use as springboards each of the eight areas in which people have problems:

Spiritual life: Is persistent sin a cause?

Thoughts: Are the person's thoughts leading directly to recurrent problems?

Table 4
Conducting a Focused Problem Discussion

Focus	Examples of Lead-ins
Problems	What are some of the things that trouble you most?
	What are your main problems now?
	What are some things you'd like to change?
	Let's try to be a little more specific. What happens when you get [feeling label]?
	Exactly what do you do when you get [feeling label]?
Priorities	Of the problems you've mentioned, which do you think bothers you the most?
	Which of these problems do you think would be the easiest to change?
	If you could change one of these right now, which one would it be?
	Let's see if we can decide what order to attack these problems. Usually it's good to start with an easy one first. Which would you like to talk about?
Goals	If things were like you wanted (or were back to normal), how often would you be doing this?
	What's the difference between how much you are doing this now and how much you would like to be doing this next month (week, year, etc.)?
	Judging by your current situation, do you think that's a realistic goal? We want you to be successful.
	Suppose you reach (or didn't reach) this goal. How do you think you'd feel?

Imagination: Are images causing negative emotions?

Feelings: Are the person's emotions consistent with the situation?

Behavior: Is this person acting in such a way that bad situations are inevitable?

Physiology: How is this person's body involved in the problem? Is he or she getting sufficient sleep? Proper diet? Are hormone changes occurring? Weight changes?

Social environment: How are the person's family and friends reacting? What effect is the problem having on intimate acquaintances?

Physical environment: What are this person's living conditions like? Can these be contributing to the problem?

Focusing Discussion

As you consider each problem area in more detail (after you have helped the person set limited, specific goals for that problem), you will continue to focus discussion on that problem. Be sure that you can describe each problem fully. What happens *before* the problem is experienced? What happens *while* the problem is experienced? What occurs immediately *after* the problem is experienced? Encourage discussion of several occasions when the problem was experienced. Most people tend to discuss problems in generalities, but discussing specific instances usually yields more helpful information about what is actually happening.

Helping your friend describe a problem fully also involves developing a clear, accurate picture of the situation. Bandler and Grinder discuss several sources of inaccuracy in the mental representations that people have of their problems.[1] A *vague, incomplete or distorted picture* can be a factor. Your job is to help them clear up such distortions and omissions. Another source of inaccuracy is *generalization;* for instance, your co-worker says, "I'm angry with the world." Recognizing this as a generalization, you can ask, "Who specifically angers you?" If the person replies, "Jim really angers me" you might respond, "How does Jim anger you?"

Another tip-off is the mention of *impossibilities*. Though someone might say, "I just *can't* say 'No' " he or she actually can say no. Therefore, you might ask, "What stops you from saying it?" or "What would happen if you said it?" or even "You mean you have never told anyone no?" A final clue to inaccuracies are *false assumptions,* sentences beginning "I know" or "I realize" or "I understand" or "I recognize." If a young man says, "I know she doesn't want to go out with me" you might gently challenge him by asking, "How do you know that she doesn't?"

In addition, you can keep the discussion productively focused by using the fruits of your thinking. If you have identified any general themes, tentatively suggest that the person consider them: "There seems to be a common thread running through much of what you have told me. It seems like every relationship that you've had since Mary jilted you has ended by your getting disillusioned with the woman and dropping her abruptly. Have you noticed that pattern?"

Another way to focus a discussion is to concentrate systematically on categories of causes. If you believe that people most often have problems because they think unproductive thoughts, then ask, in a variety of different ways, what they think about under certain circumstances. As I said in chapter two, Lawrence Crabb believes that most problems are caused because people think things that are not in accord with the Bible. Jay Adams, on the other hand, is more concerned with whether the person's behavior is biblical. The systematic focus of both of these men will direct their clients' attention to the respective areas on which they concentrate and will help them define the problem accordingly.

There are few ways to turn off a person more quickly than clumsily leading. You must instead use all the active listening skills to make the person feel understood while you guide them. Recall that most of the active listening skills necessitate a decision about how you will respond to any statement. You can choose which words to restate, what content and emotions to reflect or ignore, what questions to ask, and what you will summarize. Systematically focusing attention does not mean that every response will be directed at the cause. Indeed, you must wait patiently until the person says what you consider to be important and then reflect that. Your reflection will usually reward your friend for discussing that topic and will guide him or her to discuss it more. The whole process should be focused on what the other person initiates and not on your guiding. If the person feels manipulated, you are pressing too hard for acceptance of your understanding of the problem. There is no need to press: people live rich lives, and they will bring up the topics of interest if you wait patiently.

Equipped with new skills to rethink a problem, let us find out how Phil is.

Phil: Session 2
54-Me How was this week, Phil?

54-Phil Kind of up and down. After I left here on Monday, I felt great. I even got one of the best nights of sleep on Monday that I've had in a long time. But that didn't last.

55-Me Oh?

55-Phil Yeah. On Tuesday night I had a study date with Karen and afterward, we got into another argument about sex. That started me thinking again, and it's been back to the same old worrying ever since.

56-Me But you did have one good day.

56-Phil Yeah. And it was nice.

57-Me I wonder what you did differently on that one good day.

57-Phil Well, one thing different was that I kept thinking that at least I probably wasn't crazy.

58-Me So you *thought* something different.

58-Phil Uh huh. And I thought that really I didn't have as many problems as it seemed like I had before I talked to you.

59-Me And thinking that was a relief.

59-Phil You bet!

60-Me [Silence]

60-Phil I guess those are the only differences. I don't really know. I really wasn't thinking much about differences. I was just enjoying it more than anything.

61-Me So, maybe another difference was that you *weren't* thinking about your problems all the time.

61-Phil Right. [Pauses] Yeah. Right! I didn't think about it— hardly at all. But I've sure been thinking about it since. And I don't like it any better than I did before.

62-Me I can imagine. You know, Phil, last week I asked you to think about how you cope with your worries when they come up. I suspect that you had some opportunities to do that this week. What did you come up with?

62-Phil Yeah, I did have some chances to think about how I handled the worrying. I guess that my main conclusion is that I don't handle it very well. Mostly, I just tell myself not to worry, but it doesn't do much good.

63-Me How do you usually get over the worrying?

63-Phil Usually I just get busy doing something else sooner or later, and when I notice, I'm not thinking much about it any-more.

64-Me What about when you start thinking about it at night?

64-Phil Yeah, that's the worst. There's nothing I can do, so I just toss and turn and think until I get so worn out that I fall asleep.

65-Me So there's not much you do to try to stop worrying except tell yourself to stop, and that doesn't seem to work very well.

65-Phil Right. Do you have any suggestions? I really am tired of living with all this confusion all the time. I want to *do* something.

66-Me You know, Phil, one thing we might do is try to decide what you want to get out of our time together.

66-Phil I don't really understand what you mean exactly. Do you . . . ?

67-Me I mean it might help if we had a clear idea of what would be different after counseling than before. See, here's what I'd like to do: I'd like us to meet together a total of about five times. Then we can see what has happened and can evaluate whether we think it would help to meet anymore after that.

67-Phil That sounds like a good idea.

68-Me Well, in order to get a clear picture of what you want to accomplish over the next few weeks and to help you figure how successful you are at getting there, we need to make some clear goals. How does that sound?

68-Phil It makes a lot of sense. I know what I want. I want to not be confused and to know exactly who I really am.

69-Me Wow! That's a tall order for five weeks!

69-Phil Yeah, well, I guess it is a little much.

70-Me Let's start by having you summarize the problems that you feel are the most important or that bother you the most.

70-Phil That's easy. I feel confused all the time. I don't know who I really am. I seem to be a hundred different people all fighting each other.

71-Me So one thing you'd like to do is to get rid of your confusion, and you think that will happen if you figure out which one of these different Phils is the real Phil.

71-Phil That's it in a nutshell.

72-Me And, in particular, the times that you feel the most confused are . . .?

72-Phil Well, when I sin. And when I think about school or work. And when I'm with my roommates and their girlfriends. And lately when I'm with Karen. [Pauses] But when I do most of my worrying is when I'm alone.

73-Me So it sounds like there are three things that concern you the most. One is living a consistent Christian life. Another is deciding what to do about school or work. And the third concerns your relationship with Karen, especially the sexual part of it. Does that sound accurate?

73-Phil Yeah.

74-Me Also the times that these concern you the most are alone times, especially when you go to bed.

74-Phil Uh huh.

75-Me And what you do is worry about these things over and over, and it doesn't help to tell yourself you want to stop worrying.

75-Phil Yep.

76-Me Okay, let's try to find out how often you think about these things in a worrying way.

76-Phil All the time.

77-Me You mean every waking hour?

77-Phil No. But at least four or five times a day. I really don't know exactly. It seems like all the time.

78-Me Okay. Let's say about... thirty times a week. How does that sound?

78-Phil That's probably close enough.

79-Me Of course, it would really help to know exactly, but it takes a lot of energy to count those times, and you probably wouldn't be willing to put out that much energy. About how upset do you get when you start to worry? Let's see. Suppose you had an upset-meter that ranged from zero to ten, where zero meant that you think about these things but it has no effect at all on you, and ten means that it gets you the most upset that you've ever been. About how upset do you get when you worry?

79-Phil It's different. Sometimes I'm ten, like the day I came to see you last week. But sometimes I'm only about, oh, six or so.

80-Me So you range from six to ten. What is the average, would you say?

80-Phil About seven and a half, I guess.

81-Me Okay [pretends to write], seven point five-eight-three-six, plus or minus two.

81-Phil [Laughs] Yeah. We've got it nailed down now.

82-Me Right. Now, Phil, being realistic, what would you like to reduce the average to by five weeks from today?

82-Phil [Pauses] I guess I could live with a four.

83-Me What would that mean to you?

83-Phil Well, it would mean that I really had this thing under control and that it probably was just a matter of time before I quit worrying altogether.

84-Me And what if you didn't get that far? Suppose you only go down to six.

84-Phil Oh, I don't know. I guess it would be disappointing, but I would survive.

85-Me Good. Every week when you come in I'm going to ask you about your week, and I want you to try to estimate the average upsetness you felt that week and also about how many times you worry about these things. You might even start a graph. It could be interesting to see your progress.

85-Phil Yeah, it could.

86-Me Now, which of these things has been bothering you the most?

86-Phil Well, I guess, the . . . uh . . . sex thing with Karen. [Blushes] Of course, it's all tied up with living a Christian life too.

87-Me Tell me what happened this week.

87-Phil Well, it makes me so dratted mad at myself. Karen and I had this argument about sleeping together—and what makes me so mad is that I found out last week while we were talking that I don't really even *want* to have sex with her. I mean, I do, but I know it's wrong and that she doesn't want to. So I don't want to make her have any problems by pressuring her too much.

88-Me But you argued anyway.

88-Phil Yeah. After we went to the library, we went back to the apartment for a Coke, and Nick and Rita were back in the bedroom. So we went for a walk around the block, and we got to talking about whether it was really wrong to make love before marriage—I mean, you know, if you love each other.

89-Me And that started the argument?

89-Phil Yeah. And it's dumb. I *know* it's wrong and that God doesn't like it. But everybody's doing it. And I just hate to face Nick and Steve and tell them that I'm a virgin. It's embarrassing.

90-Me So you feel caught in the middle. You know that the

Bible says that sex outside of marriage is wrong, meaning that God doesn't like it, but you get uncertain when you actually hear of other people who are doing it.

90-Phil Yeah. It's so hard . . . I mean, I *want* to be strong, but . . . I can't.

91-Me You say you can't and yet you said that you were still a virgin.

91-Phil Well, I am, but it's not *my* fault. If Karen had said yes, I'd be over that problem in a minute.

92-Me Even though you say that, Phil, it sounds as though you are selling yourself short. Last week you said that you didn't really want to have intercourse before marriage. . . .

92-Phil Well, I don't, but . . . well, I guess the flesh is weak. So I know that if I had the chance—the real, honest-to-goodness chance—I'd probably give in to temptation.

93-Me And yet, with all the girls around who don't have the same resoluteness as Karen, you've managed to stay a virgin this long.

93-Phil Yeah, I have, haven't I? But those girls just don't attract me. Then there was the time I had a date once where this girl wanted to, uh, have sex, I mean, but, uh, but I got so drunk that I passed out. So, it's not like I was strong or something. I would if I could, I guess.

94-Me It is hard to know, isn't it? On one hand, you *think* that you *might* be weak if you ever got in a real tempting situation, which you have managed to avoid up to now by being attracted to "nice" girls or even, in desperation, by getting drunk. On the other hand, you have the absolute fact that you *are* a virgin.

94-Phil That's right, but it makes me sound stronger than what I feel.

95-Me Well, I'm not trying to do that. But sometimes you seem to be saying that you are weaker than your actual behavior indicates.

95-Phil Yeah, I sure do. I wonder why I do that.

96-Me Well, I don't know, but here's something you might want to think about. Most people have some very important questions that they ask about themselves. Of course, the questions are different at different ages. An older person might wonder whether he will be able to face death with dignity. A young woman may wonder whether she will be a good mother. For you, it sounds as if you are wrestling with some pretty important questions about yourself. . . .

96-Phil You mean whether I'm going to die a virgin?

97-Me Well, that seems to be one form that you ask the question in. But what I've heard you ask in several ways is, "Am I a *weak* person?" You also seem to ask the related question, "How much am I going to let others determine what I am going to do?"

97-Phil Yeah, I can see that. [Pauses] I guess I'm afraid I really am pretty weak, and it's safer to just go along with the crowd. So I always go along. That just proves I'm weak.

98-Me Let's see. You *always,* in all ways, go along, right?

98-Phil Well, I guess I don't *always* go along. In fact, I don't smoke, even though a lot of my friends do, and I don't do any drugs—not even grass—even though almost everybody else seems to.

99-Me Sometimes you are very firm about your beliefs, and you don't listen to others, and you're not tempted at all. But sometimes you are very tempted, and you do listen to others. What do you think accounts for the differences?

99-Phil Well, when I'm sure I don't like something, it's no problem not listening to others, but when I kinda waver and am not real sure, then I guess I get swayed by the crowd.

100-Me So, maybe this question about whether or not you're *weak* could be thought of a little differently. Maybe a better way to think of yourself is this: you are very strong when you decide something, but you're still wrestling with some issues.

100-Phil Yeah. I guess it's when I'm unsure of what I really believe that I'm tempted by other people. Like, I don't know what I really believe about sex before marriage. Well, I guess I do. No, I know what I *ought* to believe, but I don't know if I really do believe it.

101-Me What *ought* you to believe?

101-Phil Well, I know God doesn't like sex outside of marriage.

102-Me For any reason? What about if the two people love each other?

102-Phil Yeah, I know he doesn't like that either. But I still *want* to do it, if I get the chance. He surely will forgive me. It's not like it was murder or something.

103-Me What do you think God thinks of that attitude?

103-Phil I guess he wouldn't be real keen on it, would he?

104-Me I don't think he would like it. But what if you were really sincere in your repentance?

104-Phil I don't think that would make a difference.

105-Me Even if you really loved the girl and everybody else said it was okay?

105-Phil No, that wouldn't make any difference to God. If it's wrong, it's wrong—no matter who says it's okay.

106-Me It sounds like you really know what you should do, based on what God has told us in the Bible. The question is, will you choose to do what you know is true?

106-Phil Well, I sure want to do it, but... [Laughs] I started to say, "the flesh is weak," but I guess I've already convinced myself that if something is important to me, the flesh is pretty strong. So I can't really fool myself with that old flesh-is-weak argument anymore.

107-Me Good! I can see that it's getting about time for me to go to my meeting, so this seems to be a good place to end today. I wonder if before we go, Phil, you could summarize what you got out of today's discussion.

107-Phil Sure. [Pauses] I guess the biggest thing is that I'm not as weak as I thought, especially if I really care about something. I also found out that I was bothered by it. I mean, bothered by whether or not I am a weak person.

108-Me Of course that might still bother you. It seems to me that you're asking the same question in trying to decide whether or not to stay in school, and who you are going to let influence you.

108-Phil Hmmm.

109-Me [Pauses] Did you get anything else?

109-Phil Well, I got hope. It's nice to talk about these things. Somehow they seem so much more manageable when we talk about them.

110-Me That's good. Oh, another thing: we set some goals for the next four weeks.

110-Phil Oh, yeah. I'm going to try to reduce the bad feelings from about seven and a half to about four.

111-Me Right.

111-Phil Well, the way that I feel right now, that won't be hard. I feel about two right now.

112-Me That won't last.

112-Phil It won't, huh?

113-Me I doubt whether you can keep your mood there all week, but we'll see next week.

113-Phil Yeah, we'll see.

114-Me Well, I've got to be running. I'll see you again next week.

114-Phil Bye.

Putting It into Practice

Knowing how to help Phil rethink the problem and actually doing it are different matters. It always sounds so simple to me when I read about it, piece by piece, or even write about it, but during a helping conversation I often find it difficult to adhere to my game plan.

During the week, I had thought and prayed about Phil and his concerns. My original plan was twofold: first, to help Phil see that he was in control of most of his life except for a few very important questions with which he was wrestling, and second, to help Phil see that his worrying and some unhelpful behaviors were causing him distress. Identity crises are tough questions that people face in transition points of their lives, especially during their teens and early twenties, during midlife career shifts, and during early retirement. People are trying to decide what is stable about their lives and what values to retain. These values, along with the situations to which people expose themselves, will determine how they will act. Because these identity questions often occur near major turning points in people's lives, they strongly shape future behavior. Consequently, in addition to helping Phil feel more in control of his life, I wanted to discover and show Phil the questions that were important to him. Phil had mentioned sexual conflict with Karen, a decision about school and problems living a Christian life. I had no idea whether he would want to talk of one of these concerns or an entirely new one, but I knew that we had to talk about *one* concern rather than all of them in a general way which would have diffused our efforts. To prepare Phil to deal with his persistent worry, I decided to point out systematically how his thoughts were causing his distress. Finally, I wanted to set with him some overall goals that he could realistically achieve in the four sessions that lay ahead.

I began the session by asking Phil about his week (54-Me) because I knew it would be fresh on his mind and because I hoped that it would help focus the session, which it did (55-Phil). Phil, however, quickly turned the conversation away from the sexual problem and toward his persistent worry (55-Phil), so I emphasized the role that his thoughts played in his distress (see my lines 58, 59, 61, 64 and 65). When Phil asked for concrete suggestions, I did not feel that he was ready to act on the suggestions that I could have made. (I probably did not know enough to make any worthwhile suggestions anyway.) Therefore, I shifted to a suggestion that we set some goals for our sessions. I handled this shift poorly (66-Me). A better way to introduce the topic of goal setting would have been: "Well, Phil, I don't really think that we know quite enough yet to be able to figure out how to ease your worrying very much. But there is one thing that might help us get started. Sometimes it helps to know just how badly it bothers you. . . ." That would have led us to discuss goals and would have made a smoother transition than my actual response. The goal setting went as

I expected. Phil was probably too optimistic in his expectations (68-Phil), and we were able to agree on more realistic goals (82-Phil) than he had in mind before we talked explicitly about the goals. In the process of defining his goals we summarized the problems that Phil had presented thus far (my lines 73, 74 and 75) and estimated how often Phil worried (78-Me) and how badly the worrying bothered him (79-Phil and 80-Phil). We also explored what it would mean to Phil if he reached his goal (83-Phil) and if he did not reach his goal (84-Phil). I then asked him to state his chief concerns (86-Me); he chose to talk about the recent sex problem. I tried to keep the discussion focused on that issue while I suggested the understanding that I had in mind.

Beginning with a confrontation (91-Me), I got into a bad position with Phil. I told him how *strong* he was, while he expended much energy to convince me that he was indeed *weak*. I did not want Phil to tell me about his *faults*. A better strategy would have been to encourage him to tell me about his *strengths*. Contrast responses 91 through 95 with responses 100 through 106 in which Phil defends the parts of his belief that need to be strengthened (according to *my* values). The confronting nature of 91-95 makes it hard for Phil to accept my opinions. Even if he does accept them, he will probably tend to disagree with me more often on other issues. On the other hand, responses 100-106 produce determination to act (106-Phil and 107-Phil) and the belief that *Phil* had discovered something about himself (107-Phil). Finally, we reviewed the goal that Phil set. When he expressed confidence in his ability to reach the goal, I mildly challenged his confidence, hoping to motivate him to prove me wrong.

I felt that the session was reasonably successful, with the exception of the poor transition at response 66 and the confrontations in responses 91-95 which led me to present my conceptualization before Phil was ready to hear it (96-Me and 97-Me). Presenting new ideas smoothly is a very important part of Stage 2 helping. Let us now examine how to do this.

Introducing New Ideas

The purpose of Stage 2 is to help people think new thoughts about old problems. The new thoughts should lead directly to new plans for action. This rethinking can be limited in scope or encompass major dimensions of people's lives. You will help them rethink their problems so that they can take constructive action.

Renaming a situation.   To effectively rename people's ideas or situations, we do not merely substitute our words for theirs or persuade them that our way of viewing life is somehow superior to theirs. Renaming involves selecting one of the many ways to interpret a situation—the one that is likely to be the most helpful—and tentatively sharing it so that people can develop helpful action plans. Renaming is risky. People do not easily change their ways of viewing a situation. Your suggestion that a situation can be understood from a different point of view may be resisted, ignored or met with open hostility. The best way for people to accept new names for old situations is for them to rename the situations themselves. This highlights the value of Christian discipleship in counseling. When people become illuminated by a Christian world view, they often can reinterpret old experiences in its light. (This immersion in a world view is, of course, not unique to Christianity. All psychological approaches also systematically train people to reinterpret experiences from their frames of reference.) Here are some more tips for renaming effectively.

1. Timing.   Because renaming can be threatening to the other person, avoid renaming during the early portions of a problem discussion. Be careful to thoroughly understand the problem first. Also, anticipate how long you will be talking with the person, and plan most of your renaming before the halfway point. The person will often react strongly to the way you rename a situation, and effective renaming requires that the person readjust his or her thinking about an issue. This may take considerable time. Ineffective renaming can generate hostility that needs to be discussed before you go your separate ways

(Eph. 4:2). For example, suppose that you are talking on the phone and know that you must hang up within five minutes. Suddenly, you have a great insight into the cause of your friend's problems. Consider carefully its impact. How has he or she reacted in the past to your insights? Does your friend spend much time talking out new ideas? What will happen if your friend disagrees with your idea? Will you be able to resolve bad feelings that may arise? What would be the effect of not sharing your insight right now? Will it keep until you see or talk to your friend again? The wisest course of action might be to save the idea until you have more time to talk.

2. Don't jump topics.   If you suddenly have an insight but your friend is no longer talking about the problem, he or she will be unwilling to listen carefully to your suggestion. This is one of the two biggest misuses of renaming. The other is leading someone to your insight via questions (see chapter seven).

3. Say your idea tentatively.   Share your insight in the way that porcupines hug each other—very carefully. Introduce your idea by phrases such as: "This might be another way of looking at the problem..." or "I wonder if..." or "Could it be that..." or "Maybe..." or "Perhaps...." The idea is not to convince the other person that you are correct but rather to encourage the person to adopt a new way of looking at things and to own that new way.

4. Check it out.   After you have presented your idea, ask the person his or her opinion. This is often helpful, but it is necessary when you present new ideas. Because new ideas stimulate either resistance or more new ideas, your friend will likely begin to think furiously before you have finished presenting your idea. Important parts may go unheard. Check for comprehension and emotional reactions.

5. Look for reactions.   Some people react to renaming by taking the idea that you present and expanding it, using it for greater understanding of their lives. Others become angry. They might be threatened by an accurate explanation for their behavior, or they might feel misunderstood or put down. If people react angrily to your ideas, explore their reasons. The third reaction to renaming is passively accepting your idea, then continuing blithely with what they were thinking. This usually indicates unreadiness to hear the idea; you need to lay more groundwork before you present it again.

6. *Bounce back after rejections.* If you offer a new way of viewing a situation and the person thinks you inaccurate, you might at first become defensive. You have risked an idea that is "yours," and it has been rebuffed. You might feel misunderstood ("If you really knew what I meant, you'd know that I was right"), or you might feel angry or resentful ("I've been working so hard to come up with a new way of looking at this problem, and all you say is no"). These counter-reactions usually lead either to explaining again what you meant (louder and slower) or to tight-lipped silence. The proper reaction to a "missed" interpretation, however, is to first find out why the person does not believe that your suggestion is accurate. Next, accept it. Don't argue for your point of view. Finally, return to your active listening techniques to convey that you really do want to understand.

Use supporting techniques. Because renaming often creates resistance in the help seeker, helpers must develop a number of ways to supplement the straightforward presentation of new ideas.

1. *Drawings.* When I have worked with a person to create a new understanding of the problem, I often sketch the understanding in a block diagram. This makes me think clearly about the problem. When the person sees the problem concretely, it seems much more manageable than when it was a nebulous conceptualization.

2. *Metaphor.* A metaphor is a comparison of one situation to another that captures the emotional meaning of the situation. Usually a metaphor begins, "It is *as if*. . . ." For example, in chapter nine I summarized Phil's problems by comparing them to wrestlers struggling to tear each other apart, which captured the emotional intensity of his struggles.

3. Analogy. A metaphor can reflect feeling as an analogy can reflect content. An analogy is a comparison between two situations that stresses a crucial aspect. One of my favorite analogies was given by Albert Ellis in a filmed psychotherapy session with Gloria, a woman who was down on herself because of her faults. Ellis told her that being down on herself because she was not perfect was like saying that a man with a mangled arm was totally worthless because of his faulty arm. Gloria then understood how she had been getting herself needlessly depressed.[2]

4. Jokes. Humor can drive home a lesson that might be bitterly rejected if presented straightforwardly. I once had a client who reasoned that any time a girl did not fall all over him, it meant he was impotent. Psychologists call this arbitrary inference—holding a belief so strongly that every little happening confirms the belief (whether or not the evidence supports it). To confront this client with his faulty reasoning, I told him a joke which I had read in *The Dust of Death* by Os Guinness.[3] My version of the joke was this: A man rushed into the office of a psychiatrist, panic-stricken. "I'm *dead,*" he wailed. "You've got to help me."

"You don't look dead to me," said the psychiatrist. "But I sense a challenge. I'll take your case."

So the psychiatrist first set out to establish one fact: Dead men do not bleed. For six months, the "dead" man read medical tomes, physiological textbooks and technical papers. All stated the same thing: Dead men do not bleed. The man then moved into the applied part of his education. He attended autopsies, worked with cadavers and spent several days at the morgue. At last, he came to the psychiatrist and said, "Okay. Enough already. I believe. Dead men do not bleed. I know it!"

The psychiatrist smiled and slipped his hand inside a drawer in his desk. Suddenly, he leaped across the desk, grabbed the man's finger and pricked the end of it with a needle. A drop of blood oozed out and fell to the floor.

The man's eyes snapped open. He stumbled back against the wall and gasped, "Dead men *do* bleed."

This joke allowed me to present a threatening idea without arousing my client's defenses. It also made the point in a memorable way.

5. *Story.* One particularly difficult client of mine was an author of short stories. Because he was shy, he never asked women for a date. Actually, he *had* dated once at the age of seventeen, but the experience had been disastrous and he had never again ventured into the dating world. Here, at thirty-five, he felt that life was passing him by. To cut through his terror, I wrote a short story for him. It told of a man, alone in his apartment, hiding from enemy soldiers. His food was rapidly used up. He wanted to go out to find provisions, but though he had heard no sign of the soldiers for days, he was too terrified to venture outside. At last, as his strength waned, he crawled to the doorway and, after much agonizing indecision, inched it open. This startled a rat on the steps—it bolted, knocking over a broom. Petrified, the man silently closed the door, convinced that the enemy was still afoot. He crawled back across the room to await his death by starvation.

This story captured the fear of my client and the irrationality of that fear. Because truth was presented in a way that he, an author, could identify with and understand, he was encouraged to begin a closer relationship with a woman with whom he worked.

6. *Self-disclosure.* If you have experienced a situation similar to your friend, you will probably want to share your experience. Keep in mind that your experience is your own and should be presented tentatively (see chapter nine). Your aim should be to merely present your experience as another way—not *the* way—to view the situation.

7. *Homework.* Many people learn more easily by doing than by talking. For such a person, suggest tasks or activities aimed at helping him or her concentrate on a possible cause of the problem. For instance, if your friend's thought patterns are destructive, prescribe a daily recording of thoughts about a problem. Your overweight friend could benefit by keeping

track of how many snacks he or she eats each day. If a person becomes involved in homework that focuses on one aspect of the problem, he or she will usually be prepared to listen to your statement on the importance of that aspect. Suggest tasks carefully so that the person will concentrate on the part of the problem that you think is the most important.

Prelude to Action

All during Stage 2 of the helping process, you will be working with the person to look afresh at various aspects of a problem. This may continue throughout the helping process. At some point, however, you will decide that the problem has been defined well enough to launch a concerted attack. As a prelude summarize your understanding in a more organized, systematic way than you have done up to that time. Begin by stating why the person has asked for help. Follow this by stating some of the causes on which you two have agreed. Then, reassure the person that some help seems possible. (Don't make your claims too optimistic or too pessimistic.) Finally, suggest that some action seems possible.

Suppose that Marie is distraught over her inability to lose weight. She believed at first that the cause was her "fat personality." (Notice that she defined the problem so change was almost impossible: she must change her entire personality.) After talking over the problem, the two of you agreed that she try to write down what she was thinking immediately before she ate each time during the week. She did this, and the two of you have formed a different picture of her inability to lose weight. You present the understanding: "Marie, what you want to do is lose fifteen pounds before summer gets here in about two months. Is that right? . . . Okay, it seems that you've come up with the idea that you are unable to lose this weight as easily as you would like because you have trouble resisting tempting foods. Each time you see a tempting food, you think something like, 'Oh, it won't matter just this once,' or 'I'll exercise a little more today to burn this off' or 'I really am hungry.'

It looks like, then, you have a couple of ways you can beat this problem. You can try to fix your home so that you won't be tempted. Or you can try to change those thoughts that get you in trouble. I think that either or both of those plans might work to some degree if you are willing to 'suffer' a little. What do you think?'' This conceptualization summarizes the problem and the causes which can be changed. Marie is ready for action.

Meanwhile, Phil has had a week to consider his problems in a new way and to focus on what he considers the most troublesome situation. The time has come to help him prepare for his attack.

Phil: Session 3

115-Me Hi, Phil. How are you doing?

115-Phil Fine. Sorry I'm late. I had trouble finding a parking spot. I finally ended up parking up the street about a half mile.

116-Me Sometimes it's hard to find a spot.

116-Phil [Takes a seat] Well, I had a real good week.

117-Me Oh?

117-Phil Yeah, Karen and I didn't argue a single time this week, and I felt good almost all week. I think I'm getting better.

118-Me Good! I'm glad you're feeling better. Let's see. Let's take a kind of survey. Can you summarize the things that have been bothering you, even though you feel okay right now?

118-Phil Sure. When I came to you a couple of weeks ago I was superconfused. I didn't know who I really was. In fact, I still don't know much more than then, but it doesn't seem to bother me quite as much. And I've hardly been confused all week.

119-Me What accounts for the change?

119-Phil Probably the fact that I really haven't spent much time thinking about it. It's been a busy week.

120-Me So you've thought about a lot of other things and haven't really had time for worrying.

120-Phil Right. In fact, I've reduced my upsetness to *two*.

121-Me You mean on your ten-point scale?

121-Phil Yeah. Look. [Reaches into his pocket] I even kept track each night of how upset I was that day. See, I was one on Monday night, three on Tuesday, two on Wednesday, two again on Thursday, one on Friday, up to three on Saturday and three again last night. I even averaged it out. It comes out two point one.

122-Me Great! Fantastic! You did a good job. That's a lot of work.

122-Phil It was kind of fun.

123-Me Well, you did very well. [Pauses] Okay, let's go back to our summary. You've been confused and upset. . . .

123-Phil Oh, yeah, and also unsure about whether I'm weak or strong.

124-Me Okay. Let's see if we can draw a picture of your problems. Here, let me get a pad of paper. Now, I believe your situation has three distinct parts. First, there are things you believe. Let me represent that by this circle which I'll label "Known Values and Behaviors." [Refer to Figure 4 for the complete drawing.] Now, some of those values and behaviors are not really settled yet. So I'm going to represent those by this box inside the circle, and I'll call it "Questions of Concern."

124-Phil You mean, like whether or not I'm really weak?

125-Me Right. And "What do I really believe about sex, consistent Christian living and school versus work."

125-Phil And another is, "How much will I let other people influence me?"

126-Me Good. Can you think of any others that are unresolved for you right now?

126-Phil No. I can't think of any.

127-Me Okay, let me write those down right here below the circle. [Pauses while writing] Now, there are certain situations that seem to provoke you to worry about these questions. [Draws diamond and writes, "Situations That Disturb"]

127-Phil Yeah, like especially when I try to go to sleep some nights. And when I'm near my roommates and their girlfriends, or with my father. Matter of fact, all I have to do is hear from my father and that does it. I start right up worrying about school.

Figure 4
My Conceptualization of Phil's Problem at the Beginning of Session 3

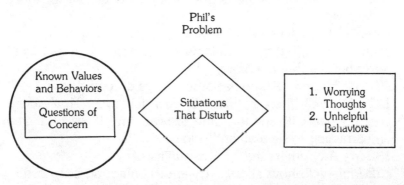

Phil's
Problem

Known Values
and Behaviors

Questions of
Concern

Situations
That Disturb

1. Worrying
   Thoughts
2. Unhelpful
   Behaviors

Questions

1. Am I a weak person?
2. What do I really be-
   lieve about:
   a. Premarital sex?
   b. Living a consistent
      Christian life?
   c. School vs. work?
3. How much am I going
   to let others deter-
   mine what I am going
   to do?

Situations

1. At night in bed
2. With roommates
3. With father
4. With others who are
   sinning
5. When unsure about
   beliefs

Thoughts

1. The flesh is weak
2. Everybody's doing it
3. It's embarrassing
4. I want to be strong but
   I can't
5. God will surely forgive
   me

Behaviors

1. Idle times
2. Getting in situations
   where people are sinning

Or when I'm with anyone who's sinning, I just seem to go along.
128-Me But last time you said that marijuana was no temptation
to you.
128-Phil Right. I guess the biggest temptation is when I'm with
someone who is sinning and I'm unsure of my own beliefs.
129-Me Now, when you get in one of those situations, you
start thinking certain things that cause you either to worry or
to sin even though you don't want to. [Draws rectangle and
writes "1. Worrying Thoughts"]

129-Phil Yeah.

130-Me What are some of the thoughts you have in those situations?

130-Phil Well, let's see. . . I think, well, the biggest is, "The spirit is willing, but the flesh is weak." Except—I guess I don't really believe that anymore.

131-Me Hmmm. And what other things do you think?

131-Phil Well, there's, "Everybody's doing it." That's been very popular with me this time of year. And there's, "It's so embarrassing to be a virgin." How's that?

132-Me Any others that you can think of?

132-Phil Well, how about, "I want to be strong but I can't" or "God will forgive me"? I could go on all day.

133-Me That will be enough for now. [Finishes writing] Now, besides worrying, you also *do* some things that makes these times bad. Can you think of some of the things that you do?

133-Phil You mean like. . . . No, I guess I don't really understand what you mean.

134-Me Suppose that you are lying in bed and you begin to worry. What do you do?

134-Phil Well, usually nothing. I just lie there and worry.

135-Me So staying idle is one thing that makes it worse.

135-Phil Yeah, and of course if I never got in those situations where others were sinning, I guess I never would be tempted either.

136-Me Good. Can you think of anything else?

136-Phil [Pauses] No. Not right off.

137-Me Okay, so here we have a picture of your problem. What do you think of it?

137-Phil It seems so simple when you draw it out like that, but it seems right on.

138-Me Good. I'll tell you what. I am going to give you this so you can look at it this week and maybe come up with some things that you might *do* to beat the problem. What do you think about that?

138-Phil Sounds good to me. It all seems to be coming together for me. I think I'm about over this.

139-Me I'm glad you're feeling so much better. But it seems to me that you are in a dangerous time.

139-Phil How's that?

140-Me Well, you're feeling better, and you've come to understand yourself a little better, but we haven't done much to plan how you are going to cope with the next crisis when it comes.

140-Phil And you think it's bound to come, huh?

141-Me Unfortunately, things don't usually go exactly the way we'd like.

141-Phil Well, okay. Maybe next time we can figure out how to cope.

142-Me Yeah. We'd better end today. I'll see you next Monday.

142-Phil See you then.

After you have helped people develop new conceptualizations of their problems, you must help them plan changes in their lives. That is where the action is in helping—in the times that the people try to handle their problems on their own. Helping people plan effective action programs requires selecting appropriate actions, giving suggestions, dealing with resistance to your suggestions and securing a commitment. In the next chapter we will discuss how to accomplish each of these.

11

Planning for Change (Stage 3)

Before you help a person decide how to solve problems (Stage 3), you should be able to describe them from his or her point of view (Stage 1), and you should have worked with the person until the two of you have developed a new way of thinking about the problem (Stage 2). That new way of thinking will lead to new solutions. Only then will you be ready to create an action plan. If you help the person make and carry out an action plan, you will not waste time on random, ineffective helping. You will get to the heart of true helping.

An Ideal Plan
If you don't know where you're going, then you probably won't get there. To "get there," you must clearly define both the goals you seek and the road you will take. The action plan

is the road to change. Most importantly, it must be a road on which your friend will travel. The most beautiful plan in the world is useless if the person does not carry it through.

First, a plan must "fit" the individual. A prerequisite is an accurate assessment of the person's "learning channel"[1] and problem-solving style. The proposal must also be consistent with each of your sets of values. If your friend is visually oriented, the plan that you construct together should include as many visual aspects as possible (such as drawing diagrams, making visual reminders of intended actions, or using objects in the person's day-to-day world as cues to action). If the person's orientation is auditory, incorporate sounds within the action plan. Simple rhymes or even alarm clocks can be used to cue action. The person might learn to relax to combat anxiety by recording relaxation instructions on cassette tapes. The person could also be encouraged to listen to his or her own thoughts and self-talk. If the person is touch oriented, action plans should be constructed which encourage the person to act and to manipulate objects in the physical world. For example, a depressed woman could make something for someone else, simultaneously benefiting herself and the other person. An anxious person could be taught deep breathing, or an overweight person could be encouraged to exercise.

Second, an ideal plan is practical and has a high probability of success. It is self-directed and self-monitored. Your friend is more likely to maintain changed behavior if he or she has some responsibility for designing the plan, for carrying out the plan and for monitoring progress. The plan that the person devises should provide for systematic movement toward stated goals. Progress should be measured in steps. In general, the first step should be easy to accomplish but not meaningless. This provides instant success and helps overcome the inertia of being stuck with a problem. It also fosters the necessary expectation that action is necessary to effective problem solving.

Third, an ideal plan revolves around one theme, but it should use as many of the eight parts of human life as practical. The theme should emerge naturally from the first two stages of helping, flowing easily from the way that you have helped the person view the problem. If you find it impossible to tie an action plan directly to your understanding of the problem, you can probably expect the action plan to produce few results. Recall from chapter three that people are composed of complex interacting systems, connected as if by springs. When a person experiences a problem in one area of life, before too long the entire person is upset. Nearly every type of psychotherapy uses the same method to help people regain control of their lives: entering the system and stabilizing one (and only occasionally two or three) of the eight parts. For instance, a behavioral therapist seeks to stabilize environments and behavior. A cognitive therapist seeks to stabilize thoughts and imagination. A cognitive-behavior modifier deals with thoughts as they relate to behavior. A psychiatrist may prescribe drugs to stabilize bodily reactions. A pastoral counselor may emphasize spiritual life. An existential therapist may concentrate on feelings.

Each therapist tries to help people regain control of their lives in one or two areas in order to dampen the vibrations in the other parts. You, too, should help your friend regain control of as many areas of life as practical. If you have a great deal of time and a close relationship you may try to work within a number of areas of the person's life. In most cases, however, your time will be more restricted and you will want to concentrate on what you consider to be the one or two most promising areas. The danger of attacking a problem on a wide front—all eight areas at once—is that you will spread your resources too thin and will be ineffective.

Designing the Plan

To want to carry out any behavior, a person must be in the right frame of mind. This is impossible without a clear rationale for the strategy including reasons why the action should help, an overview of what the action is, confirmation that the person understands what is going to happen and commitment to participate. For example, suppose a helper wanted to help a young Christian begin to have morning devotions.

Helper John, you've said that you are a new Christian, and that you really don't know much about what the Bible says. I've found that as a Christian I very often forget exactly what the Bible says. I do remember that at one point Jesus said, "Man does not live by bread alone, but by every word that comes from the mouth of God." That really seems on target for me. I eat three meals a day, but I always have to eat again the next day because my body just uses it up. I read the Bible each day because my mind seems to forget it if I don't continually replenish the supply. I think that it helps to read the Bible every day. Do you think that would be helpful for you?

John I guess so. But it kinda seems like we ought to be able to read the whole thing once and have that last us, doesn't it?

Helper That would be nice, but to keep us alive spiritually, we seem to need a steady diet. Being spiritually healthy involves deciding how much you want to take in and how often you want to take it in.

John Well, you said that you read the Bible every day. Do you think that's enough?

Helper I do try to read at least a chapter every day. But I do it because I enjoy getting to know God better—it's not that I want to fulfill some arbitrary standard. The question for you is, how much do *you* want to fit into your life?

John I guess I can start with a chapter a day.

Helper Then, if you want more, you can always increase that.

John Right.

Helper When do you think would be the best time for you to read the Bible?

John Let me think. . . right before I go to sleep each night would be a good time. I usually spend a little time unwinding about that time anyway.

In this example, the helper gives a rationale for regular Scripture reading, then allows John to make the decisions. In the process, a clear overview of the plan is given and John makes a commitment to action.

One spur to action is turning the desired outcomes that you have identified in Stage 2 into clear, measurable goals. In a simple way, that is what the helper guided John to do with his daily Scripture reading. Instead of leaving the outcome vague ("I really should read the Bible more often") the helper encouraged John to say exactly how many chapters he would try to read as well as the exact time the reading would take place. John can gauge his progress by comparing his actual behavior to those goals.

When recommending a plan, consider your experience. Have you tried the plan? Has someone you know tried the plan? Has someone whom you were helping tried the plan at your suggestion? From whom did you hear about it? Did you read about it or see it described on television? How much do you trust the source? Next, how did the plan work? Helpers often propose a plan because it sounds promising but they never put it into practice. Be especially wary of things you see on television, be they fiction or dramatizations. These shows are often written for the effect on the audience rather than with a zeal for the true effect on people. Finally, consider the person you are trying to help. Be sure that you plan according to his or her values and preferences, working logically from the conceptualization of the problem. Consider the environment, including family members and their probable reactions.

Plans come in two varieties: behavior that you try to elicit when the two of you are together, and behavior that you try to elicit when the two of you are apart. When you are together, you may want to act out what you want the person to do later ("modeling"). You might also want to have the person practice important behavior and then listen to your feedback.

Numerous plans are possible which the person can carry out between meetings with you. For example, Stella is trying to make a career decision. You could suggest that she do a field survey in which she interviews people in the job she is considering. Another friend might respond well to a system of rewards and punishments that are self-administered. This could take the form of a contract with himself or herself specifying intentions and results if the agreement is broken.

Alternative plans can be developed if you recall the eight-sided model of human experience and ask yourself what the person could do to change his or her behavior, thoughts, imagination, emotions, bodily reactions, spiritual life, or physical or social environments. Select the strategies that fit the general theme, and help the person plan for systematic change.

Suggesting the Plan

The most important part of helping is encouraging action. Your manner of suggesting action can have a vital impact on whether the person acts. Jay Haley points out that there are basically two types of directions—those that ask someone to stop doing something and those that ask someone to do something differently.[2] Asking someone to stop doing something is one of the most difficult directions to enforce. A direction to stop usually must be accompanied by other messages such as yelling, threatening or even physically preventing the behavior, as most adults who have spent any time around children have discovered. Many parents report that they seem to spend all their time following the children around saying, "Don't do this. Don't do that." A much less hectic approach is to tell the child what he or she *can* do. The same is true for the helper, who should suggest alternatives such as "Let's cook less food tonight so we won't be tempted to overeat," or "How about snacking on carrots, celery and lettuce rather than the higher calorie potato chips and candy?"

Give clear suggestions in a confident but not dictatorial manner. Be clear and concrete. Break a complex set of directions into a step-by-step sequence. Avoid generalizations. If possible, include within your suggestion what to do, how to do it and what not to do. Reread this paragraph and notice that I have suggested that you do a number of things. I have tried to describe those things concretely and have given an example of suggestion giving. Finally, check to see whether the person understood the directions or the suggestions by asking directly, requesting an "instant replay" or summarization.

Motivating for Action

Behaviorists define motivation as the response to a reward. They believe that humans usually pursue the goals they want. You can use this principle in showing people how the behavior that you suggest will lead to the ends that they desire. This is not always as easy as it sounds, especially when the person is entangled in a relationship in which his or her goals are at odds with the goals of another person. Your task is to place those rewards afresh in the person's mind, which alerts him or her to carry out the behavior. Most of us are influenced by what happens in our environment and especially by what we think right before we act. A reminder of the potential rewards of a behavior will often persuade the reluctant.

Another way to motivate people to follow your suggestions is to dramatize that past efforts have not solved the problem. Ask what has been tried. As each effort is described, ask about its success. This gently readies people to listen and to try what you suggest. Finally, you can heighten motivation to do tasks between meeting times by asking them to do tasks *during* meeting times. Once following your suggestions becomes familiar, continued acceptance is likely.

Calling for Commitment

You would think that when a professional psychotherapist assigned a client a task, the client would do it. You would think that when a physician prescribed a heart patient some medicine, that the patient would take it. But you would be wrong a surprising number of times. People often fail to do what they say they will do or what they are told to do, even if compliance can save their lives. Research on this significant problem concludes that compliance or resistance can be predicted best by the behavior of the person making the request. Therefore, if you want people to follow your suggestions, the burden is on you, not on them. *You* can help people not resist what you suggest.

One way to head off resistance is to ask the person how he or she might avoid doing the task. As the person mentions each reason, ask how it could be prevented. You, too, can mention ways that the task might be avoided. Such discussion helps the person plan how to deal with the resistance before it actually happens.

My wife, Kirby, used to direct a preschool. The rainy season in Missouri is quite muddy, so each day during the outdoor playtime the children would make a beeline for the swing set and—you guessed it—the biggest mudhole in the entire yard. Exasperated that whatever she tried did not keep the children out of the mud, Kirby asked if I had any suggestions. I was wrestling with a similar problem: my clients were not following some of my suggestions. We had carefully devised action plans —to no avail. Each week the clients returned without having done the "homework" I had assigned.

Then I came across an experiment done by psychologist Daniel O'Leary.[3] He found that children who were twice told not to cheat cheated more than those who were told not to cheat and then asked to repeat the rule. O'Leary reasoned that if saying the rule once was good, saying the rule every time a decision was to be made would be better. So he arranged a second experiment based on that principle.[4] His results were astounding. The children who repeatedly said the rule cheated only four per cent as much as the other children who merely knew the rule.

I eagerly shared these experimental results with Kirby. The next day when play time rolled around, Kirby announced to the class, as she had done on other damp days, that the swing set was off limits because of the mud. Then, however, she paused and asked, "Okay, what is off limits today?" to which the children all gleefully shouted, "The swing set is off limits today!" It worked. They stayed away from the swing set. Though my clients were adults instead of children, I applied the same principle. As before, we carefully planned actions for the clients to take during the time between our meetings. At the end of our sessions, however, I stopped and asked, "Okay, what is it you have decided to do this week?" Each person then repeated the plan that we had agreed on earlier in the session. The compliance rate for such homework went from ten per cent during the semester before I instituted the O'Leary plan to ninety per cent after I began using it.

Phil: Session 4

Phil's counseling is at a critical point. We have worked together for three sessions to develop a new way of looking at the problems in his life. In the previous session I asked him to think about what he could do to solve the problems. His situation is critical because we are about to make specific action plans necessary for change; therefore, I expect this session to be very important. As much as I would like us to immediately examine the methods of understanding his problems that we developed and to plan specific actions to correct the problems, I must wait to see whether Phil has developed any concerns this week. This is one reason that progress in helping someone is often a stop-and-go affair, lurching forward toward clear goals only to crash into a barricade of life events, then breaking free again.

My plan for the fourth session is to examine whatever concerns Phil today and, if possible, to draw him back to the conceptualization we developed. I can then help him plan action to resolve the specific concerns.

143-Me Hi, Phil. How's it going?

143-Phil Okay, I guess. [Pauses] Well, it hasn't really gone quite as well this week as it did last week.

144-Me Really? What happened?

144-Phil Well, I've been all over the place with my mood meter.

145-Me Oh?

145-Phil Yeah. [Reaches into his shirt pocket and pulls out a small pocket notebook] See, I have it all graphed out.

146-Me That's a nice little book. [He hands the book to me, opened to a small graph] Did you buy this especially to keep track of your moods?

146-Phil Well, not really. I had it lying around my room for a while. And I just decided that I might as well put it to some use.

147-Me It looks like a good idea.

147-Phil Yeah, I like it. It helps me remember to rate my moods each night before I go to bed. I just pull it out of my pocket for the next day, and I have it right in my hand, so I just think about how things have gone that day and write it down. It's worked pretty well. Except on last Thursday night. You see that I forgot to rate my mood that night.

148-Me Did something happen that night?

148-Phil Uh huh. I stayed up all night studying for an econ test. Gee, I hate that course. I mean, who cares about Keynes's theory—it doesn't work anyhow.

149-Me You seem pretty discouraged about the course.

149-Phil I guess I am, a little. I did terrible on that exam—and it's one of four exams in the course so it counts a lot too.

150-Me How bad is "terrible"?

150-Phil Oh, I don't know. About a C, I think. But, it's just . . . it's just that I studied so hard. I really wanted to do well. At least something went right that day, because then I walked into psych and got back an exam that I took on Wednesday (that's why I had to stay up so late on Thursday to study for the econ—I studied hard for the psych exam on Tuesday and worked on Wednesday night). Anyway, I got a B+ on the psych test so I felt pretty good. At least I did when I didn't think about econ. Then my parents called on Sunday afternoon. That's why you see that big spike on my mood graph. My dad makes me so mad!

151-Me So on Sunday your upsetness went way up to six or so—I can't quite make it out. Yeah, about six and a half.

151-Phil Right.

152-Me It sounds like he really "rings your bell."

152-Phil Yeah. [Laughs] He sure does that.

153-Me What happened?

153-Phil Well, I was kinda complaining about how poorly I had done on the econ exam, and Dad jumped all over me. Told me to buckle down and study, that he wasn't paying my tuition for me to be just partying all the time, that he expected some serious studying from me. I mean, gee! It wouldn't have been so bad if I hadn't spent so much time studying.

154-Me I can see that it really got you angry. Even now as you talk about it you seem to be getting all worked up again.

154-Phil Yeah, I guess I am getting a little hot about it. But, I mean, it's so unfair, that's all.

155-Me So you feel like your father just jumped on you without making any effort to understand you, and that makes you feel angry and hurt.

155-Phil Yeah. [Pauses] And then he starts . . . [Phil's voice breaks. He clears his throat and sniffs.] And then he starts to give me that old "You're-never-going-to-be-a-success" routine. It makes me want to throw up! He doesn't care about me. He just wants me to be successful so *he* can have something to be proud of.

156-Me You're pretty angry.

156-Phil I sure am. In fact, I've about decided to drop out of school and go to work full-time at the store where I work now.

157-Me You're furious at him.

157-Phil Yeah, I know. That's not really a very good reason to make a decision like that, is it?

158-Me Probably not.

158-Phil But I'm still seriously considering it.

159-Me This reminds me of the chart that we put together last week. One of the unresolved questions was how. . . .

159-Phil Yeah, "Who's going to run my life—me or somebody else?" But it's not just that. I really don't like business administration very much. And I do terrible in econ.

160-Me You say that you do terrible, but you made a C on the exam. It sounds like you have very high standards for yourself.

160-Phil Yeah, I do. That's what makes it so hard. If I can't be real good in business, then what's the use in keeping on with it?

161-Me What other practical alternatives do you have?

161-Phil I guess I could major in psych. But I don't know what in the world I'd do with it once I got a degree in it.

162-Me Well, ironically, lots of people who major in psychology for their undergraduate degree will work in business if they don't go on to graduate school.

162-Phil That's a kick in the teeth, isn't it? Anyway, I've never been much for math, and I understand that you have to take a lot of math and statistics to get a degree in psych.

163-Me That's true. You have to take two courses in stat and several courses that use the stat you learned.

163-Phil Then psych probably isn't the major for me.

164-Me What other alternatives do you have?

164-Phil None. At least as far as school is concerned. There's just one: dropping out.

165-Me You sound pretty discouraged.

165-Phil I am.

166-Me When does it bother you the most?

166-Phil All the time. Especially after the phone conversation with Dad.

167-Me You mean that triggered your worry and now you think about it in lots of situations?

167-Phil Yeah, especially when I study. You know, that forces me to think about school and work and I get going thinking about what I'm going to do. [Pauses] And then of course there's bedtime. That always seems to bring out my worries.

168-Me Always?

168-Phil Well, almost always. I start thinking and my mind just seems to go around and around over the same old thoughts.

169-Me What are those thoughts?

169-Phil Well, like what am I going to do the rest of my life? How am I going to pass this econ course? How am I going to handle my conversations with Dad if I decide to drop out of college? Things like that.

170-Me Are all of those equally upsetting?

170-Phil No, I guess the most upsetting is thinking about Dad. I just seem to have these big arguments with him over and over in my mind.

171-Me And that gets you even more upset.

171-Phil Right. I get mad every time I think about it.

172-Me Phil, what you are describing still reminds me of that diagram we've developed. In this instance, you seem to be struggling with two of the questions that we identified: how much you are going to let your father influence your life and what you intend to do about work and school.

172-Phil Right. I really hadn't thought about it in terms of that diagram.

173-Me Well, if you are going to cope with these upset times better, it will help if you let these situations spur your memory of that diagram. Then you can plan some better ways to deal with the situations than just getting all upset.

173-Phil Yeah, I guess you're right. That's why I come here. If I don't use the ideas that we come up with, then it would be better if I just stayed home.

174-Me Okay, now, you have the two questions of your father's control and of school versus work. What about the rest of the diagram? How does it apply to the things that you have been talking about today? [Pulls out diagram and shows Phil]

174-Phil Well, sure enough! Those were two situations that we said that I got upset in—talking with Dad and at night in bed. And I got upset in those situations again. Also, I'm unsure of what I want to do for the rest of my life, and being unsure was another of the situations that usually gets me going.

175-Me Good! You're using the ideas now. One thing that you said kind of triggered a thought. You mentioned that you didn't know what you'd be doing for the rest of your life. It seems that thinking about choosing a vocation for the rest of your life is a very important choice.

175-Phil It sure is. That's what bothers me.

176-Me Yeah. On important decisions like that you surely don't want to miss God's will for you.

176-Phil I sure don't.

177-Me Let me give you a little information that might help you put your choice in a *little* different perspective. Did you know that in the United States today people on the average change careers—and that's not just jobs but actual careers—from one to three times over the course of a lifetime? They change jobs within the same line of work from three to five times in a lifetime. Now, I'm certainly not trying to minimize the importance of your decision, because you will still be investing a great amount of time and energy into whatever field you choose. And, of course, we always want to be where God wants us to be, but at least you know that if you make a mistake, you will not necessarily be stuck with it for the rest of your life.

177-Phil That is comforting. I didn't realize that people changed so often.

178-Me They sure do. But, like I said, it is still an important decision. You want to be in the area that God wants you in.

178-Phil I sure do.

179-Me Okay. Now, Phil, let's go back to the diagram. Do you remember the third step, after the bothersome questions and the situations that get you worrying about those questions?

179-Phil Well, let's see. The third step was thinking things that keep me upset. Boy! I sure did that! I kept rehashing those times with Dad over and over, even though I knew that it wasn't really getting me anywhere. And those thoughts really got me worked up. I guess that wasn't a very good idea.

180-Me Well, it certainly got you upset and angry. [Pauses] Let's see, this decision about school or work is giving you trouble, and your relationship with your dad, especially over the school or work issue, is also giving you trouble. I'd like you to set some kind of concrete goal that you want to accomplish in this area.

180-Phil That's easy. I want to decide whether or not to drop out of school. If I decide that I don't want to drop out, I want to decide whether I want to continue to major in business.

181-Me Good. Those are nice, specific goals. What about your relationship with your father?

181-Phil Well, that'll probably turn out okay if I can just make some kind of decision about school.

182-Me Phil, I'd like to believe that would be the case, but I'm not as optimistic that you two will stop arguing.

182-Phil Yeah, I know. I never really believed that the arguments would stop either. We always seem to find something to fight about. Why one time when we. . . .

183-Me [Interrupts] Excuse me, Phil. What kind of goal would you like to set up about your relationship with your father?

183-Phil Well, naturally I'd like our relationship to be better.

184-Me What would that mean in terms of how you would behave toward him?

184-Phil Well, we probably wouldn't argue as much.

185-Me You've told me what the outcome would be, but what would that mean in terms of *your* actual behavior?

185-Phil [Pauses] To tell you the truth, I don't really know. I guess I'd have to think about it a while first. Maybe we can come back to it at some later time, okay?

186-Me Sure. Okay, so you've decided that you want to determine whether to drop out. How are you going to determine that?

186-Phil I don't have any idea. All my efforts seem to get me more and more upset.

187-Me Well, there are a couple of things that I know that might be helpful for you, but they might take a lot of work on your part. Do you think you're willing to try?

187-Phil Sure. Anything's better than the turmoil I've been having.

188-Me Well, first, it seems that you need to take careful stock of your abilities so you'll know what jobs you might be qualified for. How does that sound?

188-Phil Sounds good. How do I do it and when do I start?

189-Me Well, what is your schedule like this week?

189-Phil It should be pretty easy. We just finished midterms and I don't really have anything due for a couple of weeks.

190-Me Good. [I reach up on my bookshelf and take down a book.] Here is the best book about career decision making that I know of. It's called *What Color Is Your Parachute?* by a man named Richard Bolles.[5] This book will lead you through an evaluation of your strengths so that you'll be prepared to make the best decision that you can about what career to choose. It also gives you about a thousand great hints about actually landing a job. If I sound enthusiastic, it's because I am. I used to work at the Career Planning and Placement Center at the University of Missouri-Columbia Counseling Center. We kept this book available for anyone to read. The problem was that people would start reading it and would find it so helpful that they just carried it right home with them. We used to lose one of these books a week. It's tremendous. Do you think you'd like to borrow my copy and try to read it and work through it this week?

190-Phil It sounds great! You'd make a good snake-oil salesman, if that book were your snake oil. It sounds like it does everything up to and including growing hair on your head.

191-Me Well, it probably won't do that. In fact, you'll be doing all the real work. The book will just tell you about making career decisions.

191-Phil It does sound like a good book, though.

192-Me It is. I have another idea. You said that you might want to be a businessman at a store like the one you work at.

192-Phil Right.

193-Me Okay, who is in charge of the store? I mean, who holds the position that you might like to hold within about five years?

193-Phil That would be Mr. Gossett.

194-Me What do you think that he'd say if you asked to talk to him about a career in that field?

194-Phil I don't know. He's pretty busy . . . but he might like it too. I mean, I'd be showing an interest in his work. I don't know what he'd think.

195-Me Well, you know that one way to find out about the inner workings of a job is to go to a person who does that job and ask him.

195-Phil You mean, interview him or something? I'd be pretty embarrassed. It does sound interesting, though.

196-Me You sound like you have some mixed feelings about it. Maybe the best thing to do right now is to just kind of let it stew for a while and you might someday decide that it would be worthwhile to do a kind of field survey.

196-Phil Yeah, that sounds pretty good. But if I did ask Mr. Gossett for an interview, what would I ask him?

197-Me You'd like to find out about the job, of course, but it's also very interesting to find out things like what kind of background he had before getting into this business. And what kind of things he likes about his job right now. And what kind of things he doesn't like. Another good question is how he would describe the type of person who works best in a job in that field. You can then compare yourself with what he has learned and determine your probability of success. Another good question is, Where does he see himself five years from now? That'll give you some idea about advancement. What are the typical working hours? Is there any travel in the job? What type of people does he work with? What kind of job security is there?

197-Phil Whew! That's a lot to remember.

198-Me I can write it out for you if you want.

198-Phil No, that's okay. I don't think I'll be able to do it this week, but if I do I'll give you a call.

199-Me Fine. Okay, that gives you some ideas about making a start toward deciding about your career. But how are you going to cope with those worrisome thoughts if they begin to plague you at bedtime again?

199-Phil That'll be easier now that I have some concrete steps I can take.

200-Me How will it be easier?

200-Phil Well, I can remind myself that I'm making progress toward a decision even if I haven't made the decision yet.

201-Me Good. What else?

201-Phil I can think that it's not really worth missing sleep over.

202-Me Okay, I wish we had time to really plan out what you could think about in detail but we don't. Let me ask you this: what have you decided to do this week?

202-Phil I'm going to read and work through this book, and I'm going to think about whether to interview Mr. Gossett, and I'm going to battle those thoughts.

203-Me Do you think you'll really do all those things?

203-Phil Yes, I think so.

204-Me Can you think of anything that could prevent you from doing them?

204-Phil No, I can't think of anything.

205-Me What if some important assignment came up?

205-Phil It won't. I know all of my assignments for the semester and nothing is due this week.

206-Me What if you had an argument with Karen?

206-Phil Well, that would be tougher, but I guess I could still work on the book even if we had an argument.

207-Me How about any other crisis like that?

207-Phil No, I think I could still work on the book.

208-Me Okay, good. I want to do one more thing. I'd like to make a covenant with you to pray that God will lead you into his perfect will, and that he will close all the doors that he doesn't want you to go through. I want you to know that I take covenants very seriously. Kirby and I have made some covenants with people and have prayed for them every night—some for five years. And we've seen some pretty remarkable things happen with this consistent prayer. So I'd like you to know that I'll be praying for you nightly until this career decision is made. Is that okay?

208-Phil I really appreciate that. Well, I know that you're late so I'll see you next Sunday at church.

Evaluating Session 4
In this session Phil decided to resolve some of his problems.

Until this time, he had changed primarily because of the understanding he had developed *during* our times together. But lasting change will result only when he puts into effect his action plans when we are not together. This session was therefore crucial. We had to develop a plan, based on the way we had previously begun to rethink the problem; furthermore, the plan had to deal with whatever was of current concern to Phil. We were fortunate enough to be able to accomplish this.

At the beginning of the session (143-47) we checked on whether Phil was continuing to keep track of how upset he was each day. He had indeed monitored his progress and had even used his initiative to develop a way to make his record keeping easy. Phil then began to talk about the events of the past week which concerned him. He began to discuss the concern over his career choice by talking about his exam in economics (148-50), but he quickly got to an emotional topic, his interactions with his father (151-58). After he developed the account of his phone conversation with his father, I reminded him of how these events fit the new way of thinking about his concern that we had developed the week before (159). We then explored alternatives to his current career goal (161-64), and spent considerable time relating what we were talking about to the diagram of his problems (172-74). In order to reduce the emotional concern (and near-panic) that Phil was expressing, I provided some reassuring information about careers (177-78), then returned once again to the new conceptualization of the problem (179). Phil then developed some goals for dealing with his career decision (180-81). I tried to encourage him to develop some goals for dealing with his father, but he decided not to tackle that problem at this time (185-86).

Because Phil said that he did not know how to investigate different career options in ways other than those that he had already tried, I made some concrete suggestions about how he could ready himself to make an informed career decision (187-201). In the process, I tried to communicate exactly what

I wanted him to do, and I tried to be sure that he would be able and willing to do the tasks. The plans were aimed at getting information about himself (read the book by Bolles) and about alternative careers (do the field survey), thus resolving one basic conflict which was one of Phil's unanswered questions (career). Other aspects of the plan concentrated on controlling Phil's thoughts (199-201). After the plan was presented, I asked him for a verbal commitment about his actions (203), and then tried to close off resistance to the plan by trying to discuss what might cause him to not carry out the actions that he had said he intended to do (204-7). The session ended with my commitment to him that I would faithfully support him with prayer each day.

Several important lessons emerge here. First, deal with the current events of the person's life while tying these events to the conceptualization of the problem that you have developed together. Second, make suggestions that relate directly to the goals that the person has established. Third, encourage the person to follow your suggestions but do not be pushy. Finally, remember that helping is a two-way street and involves commitment from you as well as from the help seeker. Phil's problems require my availability, my thoughts and preparation for each session together, and my daily prayer support.

12

When the Plan Goes into Effect (Stages 4 and 5)

The most important part of the helping process takes place *after* the third stage of helping. In the third stage you and your friend devised an action plan for dealing with a problem. Your plan was based on a solid understanding of the person and on the new way of thinking about the problem that you and the person jointly developed during Stage 2. The most important part of helping, of course, is how the person puts the action plan into effect. The most gifted helper in the world cannot solve the smallest problem of another person: the only solution is for the person to act differently.

Even so, your involvement with the person does not end with the plan. You must be available to help evaluate the effects of actions, to lend support for further efforts to change, to follow up and to restore the relationship from one of helping to the give-and-take of friendship.

Evaluation (Stages 4 and 5)

When people try to change their behaviors, things happen. Sometimes things happen even when they are *not* trying. Changes, especially at the beginning of the helping process, are often very small. Getting over emotional problems can be like climbing a very steep hill. At the bottom, the incline is steepest and the progress is slowest; indeed, sometimes we feel we are regressing. The higher one climbs, however, the more the slope levels off until we are on level ground once again. Unfortunately, when people are in the deepest valley—when they need most desperately to clearly see their achievements—is the very time when progress is slowest and hardest to see. To help people see that they are indeed progressing because of their initial efforts to change, help them make their goals as clear as possible and help them measure change accurately. Another benefit of clear evaluation is that you, as a helper, can see whether your actions are having an effect. This is an encouragement (or sometimes an admonition). Instead of trying tentatively, unsure whether you are effective, you can be assured that you are helping.

To continually evaluate progress in helping, we need to measure specific things. We need to describe, in a measurable way, a person's status before a change is attempted. Psychologists call this "taking a base line." The more carefully people can describe their base lines, the more easily will they recognize progress. Obviously, another requisite is a clearly specified goal. People must measure how far they have progressed along the road from base line to goal and undertake various tasks that move them toward their goal.

One form of evaluation appraises these tasks. People react to assignments in a number of ways. Some do a task and find it helpful, in which case everyone is satisfied. Others do the task but do not find it helpful, in which case the task was probably not appropriate for them. A third group partially does a task and, consequently, is unclear about how helpful the task would have been if completed. Still others fail to even start a task. In the case of the last group, you need to find out the reasons. Perhaps you were partly responsible by giving the suggestion too strongly which created resistance or by giving the suggestion too weakly which left the person confused about exactly what was being asked. A more productive way to examine failure is to look for environmental pressures that prevent people from carrying out tasks. These pressures are often changeable.

People also fail to do a task or, at best, find it unhelpful when it is too difficult for them. Sometimes people so strongly desire to get over emotional problems that they set their goals unreasonably high or devise tasks for themselves that are too demanding. During the action-planning stage, the helper acts as a moderating influence to prevent this. Nonetheless, sometimes people do take on too much. In your evaluation of the task, try to discover why this has happened and try to avoid it in future assignments. Recognize also that what is appropriate for one conversation may not be appropriate for a subsequent conversation. Consider carefully with the person whether to reattempt a task. I usually discourage people from reattempting a task unless it is absolutely essential to therapy.

An important step of the evaluation process is taken after you finish trying to help the person solve his or her emotional problems: evaluating which of your actions proved helpful and which did not. Try to objectively determine whether your friend benefited from your help. This will increase your effectiveness.

Evaluation happens continually. It is not confined to any one stage, but usually is done during Stages 3 (making an action plan), 4 (support) and 5 (follow-up). It gives direction to helping and rewards both helper and help seeker.

Support (Stage 4)

Each person uses in some way the full twenty-four hours of every day. Much of that time is spent relating to other people. These relationships, of course, differ in intensity and in kind.

There is nothing wrong with that: we are finite, with definite limitations on our resources, energy and time. We each are called to live our own life—and no one else's—in a way that will glorify God (1 Pet 4:10).

The question of commitment. When a friend has a problem and seeks your help, extra demands are placed on an already full day. Regrettably, you must decide how much support (Stage 4) you can give and from what part of your life this extra time and energy will come. These are hard decisions. We can *say* that we value family above other relationships, but easily give up important family time to help others. This takes its emotional toll on us. Many counselors and pastors report feeling "burned out" after several years of helping. Often their family life suffers.

Nevertheless, since the Fall of Adam and Eve, God's standard has been that we demonstrate our love for him by sacrifice. Israelites sacrificed on altars their most valued possessions to God. God sacrificed Jesus, his only begotten Son. Jesus sacrificed his very life. Through Jesus' life and teachings and through the lives and teachings of the apostles, we learn that we still respond to Jesus' love for us through sacrifice, by pouring out ourselves for others (Jn 15:13). The standard of sacrificial love and the God-ordained value of family relationships sometimes clash, leaving us with difficult choices.

When a friend asks for your help, you must decide what level of commitment will fulfill your role as a "good steward of God's varied grace" (1 Pet 4:10). Make clear to your friend the extent of your commitment. For example, Betty has a variety of problems about which she frequently telephones you and complains. The number of phone calls has gradually increased to about five per day. You decide to set limits on your commitment to her. You could say, "Betty, I'm beginning to feel a little overwhelmed. I've been slighting my family and my work around the house lately. The pressure has really built up. I've taken a look at the things that I've been doing, and tried to see where I could reduce some of the pressures. One of the places that could be reduced is the amount of time we spend on the phone together. I love you, and I think it's important that we get a chance to talk on a regular basis, but I'm going to have to restrict the amount of time I can talk. I just can't cope with the other pressures I have. I am glad to get to talk with you each day during this difficult time, and I'll look forward to one conversation each day. How do you feel about this? Do you think you can help relieve the pressure by limiting our conversations to one per day?"

If you decide that your present commitments prevent you from supplying help, you can still be of help by being a "go between." Put your friend in touch with a professional counselor, a minister, an elder or a mutual friend. Regardless of who ultimately provides aid, your commitment should be to seeing that people's needs are being met (Acts 2:43-47; 4:32).

How to support.   One of the things that friends do best is to support each other. Consequently, you already know many ways to provide support. Here are a few of them.

Being available to listen, to talk with or to do things with your friend is very encouraging. Simply being there can help substantially. Aid the cause with encouragement to put planned solutions into effect. When action is taken, discuss the outcomes. This discussion (also called "event analysis") consumes much of the time in formal counseling relationships and is the essence of Stage 4 helping. Prayer is another means of support. Although "one-shot" prayers are certainly honored by God, persistent prayer should be offered for the person with serious emotional problems.

Provide honest and sensitive feedback about relevant subjects, focusing on the positive. Be supportive by not contributing to temptations; for example, if you invite a person who is dieting to your house for supper, keep high calorie foods to a minimum. Tangible support can also be offered through tapes, books or records that are appropriate. An especially good way to provide support is to get the person to help someone else. One reason that God allows us to undergo hardships is to equip us to minister to others in distress, as the apostle Paul explained: "Blessed be the... God of all comfort, who comforts us in all our affliction, so that we may be able to comfort those who are in any affliction, with the comfort with which we ourselves are comforted by God" (2 Cor 1:3-4). Ask for help for yourself as well.

An especially important way to provide support is noticing progress. For example, if your friend is trying to lose weight, notice and comment on the improvements in his appearance. When your depressed friend begins to appear happier, mention it. When a friend who is battling with self-control constructively handles her anger, praise her for it. In contrast, most people only receive attention for the problem. Social rewards for improving are essential to maintaining improved behavior. When people try to solve emotional problems, too often the only rewards they receive for their initial efforts are the novel feelings that accompany changes. As people continue to change, others begin to notice their progress. Some comment on this positive change, but most are too reluctant to say anything. After the stage during which change is maintained by social rewards, people will be rewarded by achieving the goals they have set for themselves. Finally, they will be rewarded by seeing lasting improvements in their lives. All of these steps are necessary for changes to be permanent. The later stages may never come, however, if people are not encouraged by social rewards early in their struggles.

Now my chance has come to help Phil evaluate the changes he is making, provide support for future and sustained change, and decide the next step for our helping relationship.

Phil: Session 5

In the last session, Phil made several action plans. This week's meeting will determine how those plans worked, providing, of course, that he put them into effect. My plan for the session is to continue to relate the events of Phil's life to the picture of his problems that we developed during earlier sessions. I hope that Phil will have tried to put his action plans to work and thus will have very pertinent events to discuss. Where the session goes will depend on Phil's behavior during the past week and on the feedback he received for his behavior.

209-Me Hi, Phil. How's it going?

209-Phil Hi, Ev. It seems pretty good.

210-Me That's got a good sound to it.

210-Phil Yeah. I tell you, I've had a super week. Easy. No tests and not much homework. I've had a lot of time to get a lot of thinking and talking done. It's been so-o-o fine.

211-Me You sound very relaxed and loose. What kind of thinking and talking did you get done?

211-Phil Well, I am loose. Look here. [He reaches in his shirt pocket and takes out his notebook, flips it open and searches for a particular page] Here. Look at this graph of my mood. That shows how loose I am.

212-Me Wow! All zeros and ones. It must have been a very good week.

212-Phil I'll say. I made a number of important decisions this week.

213-Me For example?

213-Phil For example, I worked through that book, *What Color Is Your Parachute?* What a dynamite book! It gave me a lot to think about. Most of the stuff I already knew, but it helped me put it all together. And it gave a lot of information about how to get a job. But more than anything, it got me all charged up to make this career decision. That's why I called you on Wednesday morning.

214-Me Did you get to interview your boss last week?

214-Phil Yep. It was amazing. God must have had it all planned. After I got those questions from you, I called up Mr. Gossett and asked if I could talk to him sometime soon. Well, he just invited me right over. I didn't even have time to get nervous. It all happened so fast.

215-Me Sounds like you're pretty excited about it. What did you learn?

215-Phil I had been praying hard all week about my career, and I prayed especially hard as I drove over to Mr. Gossett's house. So I guess it really shouldn't surprise me that he seemed to have all the right answers.

216-Me Like . . . ?

216-Phil . . . like his view was that I would be stupid if I didn't go on and get the degree. He said that he's seen a lot of talented people stopped short, unable to advance just because they didn't have that piece of paper.

217-Me So he recommended that you finish college.

217-Phil Well, not really. He never really recommended anything. He was real careful to say that it was my decision, but he definitely let me know that his experience indicated that if I went on in sales, I needed a degree. But he really didn't try to push me into his mold.

218-Me But it sounds as if what he said was very helpful.

218-Phil Yeah. You know it seems like he said exactly what I wanted to do all along.

219-Me What's that?

219-Phil For one thing, that I don't have to get all As. I mean, it's important to have pretty good grades, but it's not life or death, you know?

220-Me Uh huh.

220-Phil Oh, that reminds me. You know that econ test that I was all upset over last week? Well, I thought you'd be interested to know that I ended up getting a B+ on it. Can you believe it?

221-Me Great!

221-Phil Thanks. It was a hard test. I really didn't do very well, but neither did anyone else. So he curved the grades, and I ended up okay.

222-Me That certainly was a load off your mind, I bet.

222-Phil It sure was.

223-Me Getting back to the visit with Mr. Gossett. . . .

223-Phil Yeah, sorry. Anyway, after I talked to him, I went home and did a lot more praying. One thing kept coming back to me. Like you said last week, it's an important decision, but people *do* change jobs. So it's not like I'd be stuck forever in the job. Finally, I got a strong sense of peace about it and felt that I was supposed to stay in school and stay as a business major. I think I am doing what God wants me to do, but I'm still praying that if I'm making a mistake, then he'll let me know. Karen thought I'd made a good decision too. What do you think?

224-Me I think that you went about it exactly right—seeking diligently after what God wants for your life, then taking the responsibility to allow him to speak to you through your interview with Mr. Gossett. That gives me a lot of confidence that you've come up with God's solution for your life in terms of a career.

224-Phil Good. I feel confident that I'm on the right track. I think I was a little off track there for about the last six months or so. I've kinda been going my own way and leaving God out of the picture. I think, though, that I've changed that now.

225-Me It's a good feeling, isn't it?

225-Phil It sure is. [Pauses, thinking] You know, it's had a big effect on my whole life.

226-Me It? You mean. . . .

226-Phil I mean getting back close to God after being away for a while. I think I've got my relationship with Karen pretty much straightened out now too.

227-Me How so?

227-Phil Well, we spent a lot of time talking this week. We . . . uh . . . agree about what's okay and what's not about sex, I guess. We decided that neither one of us want to have sex before we're married—I mean, if we *ever* get married, that is.

228-Me So you think you have that pretty well worked out, huh?

228-Phil Yeah, I think so. We prayed together about it, and I believe we agree on what we can do . . . I mean, you know, how physical we can be.

229-Me That's good. It's nice to have an understanding about it. It takes some of the pressure off.

229-Phil Huh? Oh, I guess I never thought of it that way, but, yeah, it does kinda take some of the pressure off. [Silence] I wish all things were as easy.

230-Me I don't quite understand what you mean.

230-Phil I mean . . . I still don't know exactly what to do about my relationship with Dad.

231-Me You're still upset because he doesn't seem to understand you.

231-Phil Right.

232-Me What have you done about it?

232-Phil Nothing.

233-Me Nothing? Let's see, how much has your career decision bothered you this week?

233-Phil None, but I don't see what you. . . .

234-Me How much has your discouragement bothered you this week?

234-Phil Almost none.

235-Me Why have these not bothered you this week? They used to bother you a great deal.

235-Phil Oh. I think I see what you are getting at. You mean that I haven't been bothered by the career problem or by my depression because I've worked on how to solve them. So I've been focusing on the good things and not worrying about problems.

236-Me Exactly.

236-Phil Yeah, but I can't make anything good happen in my relationship with my dad because we just argue too much.

237-Me Well, it is true that you can't really control what *your father* does or says . . . [Pauses]

237-Phil But you mean that I can control what *I* do and say?

238-Me And even more specifically, you can control to some extent what you think about.

238-Phil Right. I see now that we've really been over this before.

239-Me And you see how it works: when you concentrate on

how bad a problem is, it just keeps you upset. But if you concentrate on how you might solve the problem, you feel a lot better, *and* you stand a better chance of actually solving the problem.

239-Phil Yeah, but what can I do?

240-Me I don't know. It must be frustrating for both you and for your father. I know he must really care for you or he wouldn't get so upset with you at times. You know, if he didn't care about you, it wouldn't matter what you did. So I know that it's frustrating him as much as it is you. Maybe you can change your thinking about the times that he "jumps on you."

240-Phil What do you mean?

241-Me You could think different things to yourself when he jumps on you than you think to yourself now. For instance, what kind of things do you think about when he jumps on you?

241-Phil I don't really know.

242-Me Okay, let's do this. I want you to imagine that your parents have just called you up. You've been talking a while and your father says, "Phil, have you buckled down and studied those business courses like I told you?" Now, what kinds of things would that make you think about?

242-Phil Well, I feel like throwing my B+ in econ right in his face.

243-Me And what else do you think?

243-Phil I think something like, "What do you mean, 'like I told you'? I didn't study because you told me to. In fact, I studied for that test long before you called."

244-Me I can see that you are already getting angry by just imagining what you would think about. Do you see how it's working? Whatever you think about is going to control how you feel and how you act.

244-Phil Yeah, you're right. I was getting all hot just thinking about it. But what you said was so right. I mean, that's exactly like Dad might say it. He just assumes that he's running my life.

245-Me But you know that he really can't run your life any more than you can run his.

245-Phil Right.

246-Me And you also know that he loves you or he wouldn't even ask how you were doing. It's just like the way you love him; you want him to know that he has developed a son that can think for himself and make responsible decisions without being told.

246-Phil Right.

247-Me Well, if thinking those other thoughts while you were imagining talking to your father got you angry, then how do you suppose that you could keep from getting angry?

247-Phil I guess I could keep from being angry if I thought different things.

248-Me What kind of different things?

248-Phil I guess I could think that it doesn't really matter what he thinks, that I'm not any less independent regardless of what he says.

249-Me Great! What else could you think?

249-Phil Probably I could think that he doesn't mean to make me mad. Like you said, he doesn't like it any better than I do.

250-Me Anything else you could think to keep yourself from getting angry?

250-Phil I can't think of anything right now.

251-Me It might be a good idea if you sit down when you get some time and try to come up with some thoughts that you could use to keep your temper under control. The more specific you are in planning those thoughts, the easier it will be for you to avoid those unproductive fights with your father.

251-Phil You're probably right.

252-Me When do you think that you might have time to plan out these thoughts?

252-Phil I guess I could do it as soon as I get home from here.

253-Me Is there anything that you can think of that would prevent you from doing it?

253-Phil No.

254-Me Good.

254-Phil You know, I *have* been thinking new thoughts, and it really has helped. Like, for instance, I didn't really do any worrying to speak of this week because I really was practicing controlling my thoughts.

255-Me How so?

255-Phil I would simply ask myself why I was getting so upset. Then I would think that there really wasn't any reason to worry because this was an easy week, and there wasn't any pressure. It also helped to be thinking about that book I was working through—the *What Color Is Your Parachute?* book. My notebook helped, too, because it reminded me all the time that I should be thinking about other things than worrying.

256-Me It sounds like you are doing just great. You seem to be knocking off those goals that you set up. Your bad moods are way down. You've made a career decision and decided to stay in school. You seem to have worked out the trouble spots in your relationship with Karen. And it sounds as if you have a much clearer idea of who you are than you did a month ago. I can tell that you are very happy about all those improvements, and I rejoice right along with you.

256-Phil Yeah, it's amazing to me that it was only about a month ago that I came to talk to you for the first time. I really was a basket case that day for sure. I feel like I've come a long way. I want to thank you for what you've done to help.

257-Me You're welcome. But, Phil, I don't believe that I've done very much. I've just talked with you and made a few suggestions. Really the change has come about because you have been willing to do things differently and to take risks. And the real changes started happening when we both started praying in earnest. God really is a good God, isn't he?

257-Phil He sure is!

258-Me I really hope that this is a lasting change in your life, but I wonder if you haven't progressed a little too fast. I mean, a month is very fast. You might even start to have some problems again. What will you do if that happens? How will you cope?

258-Phil I always have my little book. I can always go back to my mood meter.

259-Me How else?

259-Phil I still have the diagram you made up. I posted it on my cork board above my desk. Also, I've learned some things about what I think about—so I can just start doing those again.

260-Me It sounds as if you have learned a lot during the time that we've been meeting together. I think we're ready to put some time between our meetings. How about if we schedule a short meeting for three weeks from today, just to check that everything is going okay?

260-Phil Sounds fine to me.

261-Me Great. If anything comes up, you can always call or see me at church.

261-Phil Right. I'll see you here in three weeks.

Evaluating This Session

Because Phil was especially courageous at taking risks and at trying out my suggestions, this was a very positive session. He had continued to keep track of his moods, which gave him regular feedback that he was getting over his worries. In addition, he expended enormous effort to work through the book he had borrowed and conducted the field interview with his boss. His mood was helped by his unexpectedly good grade on his economics exam (220). But the most important change was his rediscovery of God's power in his life (224-26). This led directly to an improved relationship with Karen (228). The area of most concern to Phil was his relationship with his father. My strategy was to relate that problem back to the conceptualization that emphasized that he was in control of his own thoughts and behavior and could only affect his father by behaving and thinking differently himself (233-39). To help Phil experience (instead of merely hear about) how his thoughts influenced his emotions I had him imagine a situation with his father (242). Then I asked Phil to come up with other ways he could think about the situation (247), which led him to use the model of his problems. I then suggested that he try to plan exactly what thoughts would help him control his temper. This suggestion followed the guidelines of chapter eleven. My final intervention of the session (260-61) was aimed at terminating our helping relationship and restoring the give-and-take of friendship.

Follow-Up (Stage 5)

The term *follow-up* usually stimulates thoughts of what happens after we finish our helping contacts with a person. This is indeed an important part; follow-up, however, is done throughout the helping process. You must follow up the way the person describes his or her experience during Stage 1. You must systematically follow up the way you help the person rethink the problem (Stage 2) so that a clear, new conceptualization of the problem is developed. You must also help the person develop an action plan that will produce lasting change and follow up to see whether the person actually puts the plan into effect (Stage 3). Your follow-up is continuous as you support efforts to change (Stage 4). Finally, you must follow up the person's progress after your "official" helping concludes.

Short-term follow-up. The biggest concern in the field of counseling today is not whether counseling helps—we know now that it usually does. It is not even what type of counseling helps best—most well-known techniques are very effective. The most important question is, What counseling techniques encourage permanent changes? To answer this question, let's look at helping from a different point of view.

Why do people do what they do? Some counselors believe that behavior is controlled by thoughts. This does not imply that people carefully think about every action; we often act by reflex or habit. Some thoughts, however, flash through our minds just prior to almost any action. But what controls these rapid thoughts? Psychologists believe the answer lies in what catches our attention. Two things compete for our attention: what happens in the environment and the mental structures that are activated. My mental structures are enduring parts of my mental life and can include ways that I label myself, my values, my standard ways of solving problems, my knowledge, my agenda and my habitual ways of construing problems or situations. My mental structures and environmental events battle constantly to attract my attention and govern my thoughts which, in turn, govern my behavior.

For example, recently I was lying on my bed preparing a lecture. In walked my four-year-old daughter, Christen, who began to describe some of the happenings of her day. Environmental events—the presence of my books and notes, and Christen's talking to me—were in competition with each other and with some of my mental structures. One mental structure was an agenda: "I'm busy. I have to get this lecture prepared for tomorrow." Another mental structure was a value: "It's important to listen when my wife or one of my children talks to me." My books and notes prompted one mental structure; Christen's talk prompted another. My thoughts seesawed: "What's she talking about? Oh, playing on the swing. That's not important. I've got to get this lecture done. Let's see, where was I? . . . Oh, is she still talking? Maybe I'd better listen again. Still talking about playing in the yard. But that's important to her. And what's important to her is important to me." I laid aside my lecture notes and closed my book. Patting the bed beside me, I invited her up. She climbed up, continuing to talk all the while.

Suddenly she stopped in midsentence and said, "You like to listen to me, don't you, Daddy." It was more a statement than a question.

"I sure do," I replied.

"I'm glad," she said.

Two environmental events competed for my attention. Both activated mental structures that led to my thinking certain thoughts. Christen's presence and her insistent talking were strong environmental events—stronger than the presence of my books. Christen controlled my attention and my thoughts and, finally, my behavior. Professional counselors try to do the same thing when they see clients. They try to form intense helping relationships so that what they say will be deemed important. Then counselors use techniques refined through years of use, engaging the attention of their clients. Thus, all through the time that clients attend counseling sessions they are influenced to think differently than before counseling.

But what happens when a person stops going to counseling? The answer depends on what the counselor did during counseling. If the counselor was unable to induce the help seeker to make changes in the structures of his or her life, then the ground gained is soon lost. If the client made these necessary structural changes, however, then changes will more likely be maintained. Structural changes in the environment are introduced when an overweight man removes all tempting snacks from the house, or when a woman with a drinking problem decides never to bring any alcohol into the house and rearranges her driving routes to avoid liquor stores. These changes can be as simple as leaving a Bible on the pillow as a reminder to read it before going to sleep at night. They can be as complicated as changing the structure of interactions in a family that has a member suffering from schizophrenia.

Changes in mental structure are enacted when a teen-age boy begins to view himself as competent rather than incompetent or as likable rather than unlikable, or when a couple reaffirms that marriage is worth working to preserve rather than believing that tensions indicate "we're not right for each other." Mental structure changes can be as complex as adopting a new strategy for solving problems, or as simple as learning new information. Yet another change could take place in the way we look at a certain situation; for instance, instead of viewing her husband's nagging as distrusting and lamenting that "he treats me like a kid," a woman could see his behavior as concern for her welfare.

In short, changes that last will change the environmental or mental structures in a person's life. The same should be true for the help that you provide your friends, especially as you jointly develop an action plan. Then, when your friend makes changes, you can tie them to your friend's mental or environmental structures. To follow up ask your friend what happened when he or she attempted each change. Look carefully at the events of the person's life. Point out how this change applies to the other topics you have discussed. Give other examples of how this new behavior could be used. Following up each event is time-consuming. In fact, event analysis probably occupies more time than any other counseling activity.

In one sense, a helping relationship never ends. We continue to help our friends, and they continue to help us. But a person with an emotional problem probably will be in the position of "helpee" for a relatively long time. Once this phase of a relationship draws to a close, restoring the relationship to its "pre-problem" days would seem easy. Sometimes it is, but more often than not there is a resistance. Helping relationships sometimes continue even when the person has long since solved the original problem. One reason for this is that the sharing of problems often fosters a warmness and intimacy not present in the relationship prior to the problem. Terminating the helping relationship endangers that intimacy. Many people would rather bring up new problems to discuss than risk losing the intimacy.

The second reason is that helping sets up certain unspoken "rules" for how people talk with each other. Over time we "agree," without ever talking about it, that certain types of interactions are allowed and other kinds are prohibited. Both members of the friendship will try hard to keep the relationship from changing. This means that once you have helped a person solve an emotional problem, both of you would try to continue the relationship as it is. Suppose that one day you decide that Pete has solved his problem and does not need any special help. When you pose this idea to him, you may find that within a week of so, he will have developed a different problem that requires your help. Thus, you are invited to continue the helping relationship. On the other hand, if Pete says that he believes no further help is needed, you may be tempted to respond,

"Oh, really? But you don't really seem to have *completely* solved the problem yet." This attitude might show in your behavior, inducing him to doubt his opinion that no further help is needed. It is difficult to shift to a give-and-take from an I'll-give-and-you-take relationship.

Five steps can help you make the shift back to a two-way relationship. The first step is to point out Pete's achievements. Obviously, he has begun to act differently and has regained some control over his life. Recall these experiences to his mind. Second, openly share your positive feelings about his courage in daring to change and about the good changes that have happened. Stress the actions that Pete has taken. Lasting change is not difficult to notice because it almost always takes place through a person's actions. This leads directly to the third step: minimize your part.

If you have helped Pete rethink his problem and make action plans to solve it, you may want to have some credit for your part. Resist the urge to accept his praise. Why? The truth is that no matter what you do as helpers, you cannot effect lasting change in another person; talking about change does not produce it. You can honestly say that, although you had a part, change could not have occurred unless Pete had acted. You should also minimize your part because by doing so, you will help Pete maintain the changes. A branch of social psychology, attribution psychology, says that people continually try to figure out what causes changes. If Pete attributes the cause of his change to someone or something outside himself, the change tends to disappear as soon as he is not in that situation. On the other hand, if Pete realizes that the change came about from God's working in him and from his faith to trust God to provide new experiences, the change will last.

Fourth, shift the relationship to a two-way exchange by planning explicitly for follow-up. You might begin by spacing your discussions about the problem. For example, suggest that you and Pete spend an evening at an activity during which you agree not to talk about the problem. Later, you might agree to go two weeks without talking about the problem. Finally, you might agree merely to have a check-up time in several months. In short, don't alter the relationship in one big step; ease into the change. Fifth, ask him to help you in some way so that sharing becomes the norm. Request prayer, or even assistance in repairing a door. Any chance for Pete to serve you by helping will solidify the relationship as one in which you both can give and receive help.

Long-term follow-up. The major assumption of this book is that you will be called on to help friends with whom you have enduring relationships. Unlike professionals and clients in a therapeutic relationship, you will continue to live in a community with your friends after your helping tasks are finished. Unlike the helping relationship formed when a person whom God has gifted as a healer helps a person in one dramatic meeting, your relationships may not be vehicles for God's speedy grace. They might be if that is God's will for you and you accept it.

This book aims to help you minister to others over a series of contacts when that is appropriate; it is built, however, on the assumption that you will follow your friend's life over a period of time. Part of the love to which we are called is caring for others, taking care of or giving comfort when he or she hurts. It means caring about what is happening. If we care, we will ask. Reopening sensitive areas can be difficult, so it is easy to avoid follow-up. But if we act sensitively, asking the other person how he or she is coping with a former problem area will move us into a still closer relationship.

Evaluate yourself. One of the toughest parts of helping others is to look objectively at our own helping efforts. We always want to help other people, and we act in ways that we think will be the most helpful at the time. When people are talking about problem areas which might touch our own emotions, however, sometimes we do not act in the most helpful ways. Consequently, we are obliged to review our helping contacts and think about which of our techniques were helpful and which were not. We need to be tough-minded in our self-evaluations because we so easily deceive ourselves. Above all, we must pray that God will shine his light of truth on us as we evaluate. We must listen carefully to reaffirm continually that God is calling us to help others. Only if we are within his will can we give truly effective counsel.

Phil: Session 6

In the three weeks since our last session, many things could have happened. Phil might have coped marvelously with the events of his life, he might have failed miserably or his behavior could have been anything in between. My task in this session is to review how Phil is doing. Because we are moving toward a two-way relationship and away from a helping relationship, my main worry is that we will fail to move to a mutual friendship. Therefore, I must be alert to avoid helping Phil on any problems he brings up unless they truly are unsolvable by him alone. I also want to solidify his gains by pointing out the changes that he has made in his mental and environmental structures.

262-Me Hi, Phil. Good to see you looking so good.

262-Phil Hi. It's good to feel good.

263-Me How have things been going the last couple of weeks?

263-Phil Real well. Look. I'm still keeping it. [Shows me his data book] You can see for yourself that things have been going okay.

264-Me It looks nice.

264-Phil Yeah, you can see that I had only one bad period for a couple of days. But the nice thing is that I was able to handle it even though I got a little down.

265-Me Great! How did you handle it?

265-Phil Well, I tried to get my mind off the worries by doing other things. Like I rounded up a bunch of guys for some basketball, and that got me so tired out I couldn't have stayed awake to worry if my life had depended on it. I also kept telling myself not to get back into the habit of worrying, but to think positively.

266-Me It sure sounds like you've learned to cope with those moods.

266-Phil I'm still not 100 per cent confident, though.

267-Me You sure did a good job that time. How's your school work been going?

267-Phil Pretty good. I've been making As and Bs regularly lately.

268-Me I bet that's a really good feeling.

268-Phil It sure is. It helps to have made a decision. Even though there is really no difference between the courses I'm taking now and what I was taking before, it *feels* like all the difference in the world. I have a direction that I'm heading in.

269-Me Good.

269-Phil Karen and I have been doing real well too. We've had nothing but great times—no arguments or anything.

270-Me That makes it a lot more pleasant, doesn't it?

270-Phil It certainly does. [Pauses] Of course, my dad and I haven't been doing so slick. We always seem to butt heads.

271-Me That's hard for you, isn't it?

271-Phil It is. I don't like to fight with him.

272-Me Well, it's hard to break up patterns like that with our own family members. We've practiced those patterns of communication for a long time.

272-Phil Yeah, I know. But I wish we could stop fighting.

273-Me What are you trying to do to keep from fighting with him?

273-Phil I try to think that he doesn't mean to hurt me, and that he really does care about me. But sometimes he has a strange way of showing me. I also try not to be openly rebellious. I'm trying. I really am. But it doesn't seem to do any good.

274-Me I can see how it would be discouraging for you to put that effort into avoiding fights and find that the effort *never* pays off.

274-Phil Well, I wouldn't say that it *never* pays off. I mean, I think we have avoided some fights that we might have had a month ago.

275-Me But it doesn't pay off very often at all.

275-Phil Even that seems a little too strong. It does seem to work sometimes—just not all the time.

276-Me It sounds as if you are making some progress even though you have a way to go yet. I'm confident that some day you will just kind of wake up and realize that your relationship with your father is much improved.

276-Phil I wish I could be so confident, but I can see some improvement already.

277-Me Great! You know, as I look back over where you've been the last couple of months, I see quite a few changes. You've made some important decisions and in the process shown a lot of courage in taking risks. I think that you have discovered a great deal about who you are in the course of making the hard decisions that you've made. And I bet you've learned a lot about how trustworthy God is. You also seem to have developed some real character strength as attested by the fact that you coped so well with that low mood about a week ago. You look like you are doing well.

277-Phil You sound like my fan club.

278-Me You do seem to be doing well, though.

278-Phil Thanks.

279-Me As far as I see, I've done all that I can do in terms of helping you. You seem able and willing to help yourself and are, with God's help, doing a good job of it. Before you go today, though, I want to ask you to do a favor for me.

279-Phil What's that?

280-Me Would you be willing—I know it's a lot of work—to contact the college people at church and find out whether they would be interested in having a Sunday-school class just for them? I don't know many of them very well, and you could probably get a better reading of their true feelings than I could.

280-Phil Sure, I'd be glad to.

281-Me Thank you. I'd really appreciate it.

281-Phil Is it okay if I let you know in about two weeks?

282-Me Sure.

282-Phil I'll have it for you then.

283-Me I've really enjoyed the times we've been able to talk. I'm looking forward to spending more time with you in a less formal atmosphere.

283-Phil I've enjoyed it too. I'll see you at church on Sunday.

Evaluation Time
The final session. This session went largely as expected. Phil had maintained his improvements in almost every area. The one area in which he was not satisfied was his relationship with his father. When he mentioned this (270), he presented an invitation for me to help and thereby continue our familiar relationship. My response to his concern was threefold. First, I tried to empathize with him. Second, I assured him that he was behaving in a way that held some promise of success. Finally, instead of trying to convince him that he was doing as well as could be expected, I made it seem that he was doing worse than he was (274). This forced Phil to convince me that he was doing well instead of poorly (274-276). I ended by summarizing some of the changes that Phil had made and by asking him to help me in a task that I found difficult.

All my helping contacts. Two types of evaluation are needed. I must be concerned with the *outcome* and the *process* of my helping efforts. My evaluation is that Phil has made some important changes that will probably last. He has dropped his concerns over his identity largely by solving underlying problems. These resolutions involved making a career decision, agreeing with his girlfriend about their sexual relationship and restoring his relationship with God. Little progress was apparent in his relationship with his father. Therefore, at this point my contacts with Phil are not exclusively positive. His relationship with his father may improve over time; it may not.

I believe that Phil will maintain the gains he made during our time together because he significantly changed some of his mental structures. For example, he seems now to view himself as someone who can cope with bad moods rather than give in to them. He also made changes in the environmental structures in his life. For example, he and Karen made a specific agreement about expectations for their relationship. Phil also made a clear decision about his career plans. The final outcome is mostly positive.

My effectiveness in the five stages of the helping process varied. I believe that I got a good idea of Phil's concerns from his point of view during the first and second helping sessions (Stage 1). Throughout the six sessions I continually gathered information about how he perceived his world, demonstrating how understanding is continuous.

My behavior during Stage 2 (helping Phil rethink the problem) was the most variable. The way in which I tried to help Phil understand his problem was never a strong, integrated conceptualization, and I did not present it convincingly. Evidence of this was the constant reminders needed for Phil to use the model. When a conceptualization is apt, there is usually little need for review. With Phil, however, even in the last sessions I had to remind him about the model. The action plan that we created was probably my strongest contribution, as evidenced by Phil's use of the plan to his advantage. I believe that he failed to follow my suggestion to consciously change his thoughts because of my weakness in Stage 2. I did not fully convince Phil to consciously think new thoughts.

My support of Phil was fairly typical of that offered to a friend who is not a close friend or relative. Almost all of the techniques that I used would be applicable for even the closest friends, though. The follow-up that I will do with Phil will be made possible by our continual contact at church. Church activities will provide numerous unobtrusive opportunities to check in with him. Had there been no such structure, I would need more ingenuity to find common meeting grounds.

13
The Adventure of Helping

You have come to the end of your journey through this book. Take a few moments to reflect on your travels and review the highlights.

In chapter one, you began by taking a rough base-line measurement of some of your helping skills prior to reading the book, using the case of "Jim." After that, I discussed Christian helping and concluded that it involved helping that is done by a Christian who adheres to Christian assumptions, who relies on Christ to be the center of the helping relationship and who uses whatever knowledge God has revealed. In chapters three and four I presented my assumptions about what usually causes emotional problems and how to view the helping process. People were seen as complex, many-sided beings who live in social and physical environments. I find it most helpful to think of people's thoughts, imaginations, emotions, physiology, behaviors and spiritual lives. Other helpers emphasize other ways to think about human wholeness and complexity.

I view helping as a five-stage process which is applicable to anyone's theories of helping. Part two of the book systematically examined each stage. Because friends are usually sought for help because they are understanding, accepting and genuine,[1] I talked extensively about Stage 1 (understanding). Separate chapters dealt with understanding communication in general, understanding emotional expression, understanding how not to communicate, understanding how to communicate and understanding what the person believes the problem to be. I also included chapters on how to help friends solve their problems, encouraging you to help your friend rethink the problem, plan for action and be supported to attempt change. Throughout the second part, I discussed how to behave as a helper during each stage.

In chapter one you read about Jim and answered questions about how you might help him. I hope you saved your answers. I have repeated both the description of Jim and the questions. After reading about him, answer the questions again and compare your two sets of answers. You will see a remarkable improvement.

Jim (Revisited)

Jim, a twenty-six-year-old at your church, talked with you last week for about twenty-five minutes. Jim is discouraged. He is the only Christian in his office. All of his so-called friends give him a hard time about being a "Jesus freak." They say he is stupid to fall for that religious stuff. He has been under considerable pressure from his girlfriend, who is not a Christian, to stop attending church. He confesses that some sins that bothered him before he became a Christian have reappeared. These include anger, bitterness, bad language and gossip. He also mentions a "sexual sin" but seems too embarrassed to talk about it. Jim complains of often being nervous and scared.

He also has a poor appetite and wakes up early, unable to get back to sleep because his "mind is whirling." He feels low and discouraged. Last week, as he talked of being low, you saw tears in his eyes although he controlled himself with some effort. He says that he is afraid that he is going to "lose it" if something does not change soon.

Write down how you might help Jim over the next few weeks. Include (a) anything else that you would like to know about Jim, especially what you would ask him the next time you talk, (b) what you think his biggest problem(s) is (are), (c) how you would like Jim to think about his problem(s), (d) what goals you might have for him, (e) what you would try to get him to do about his problem(s), (f) how you might accomplish this and (g) how you would know whether you were successful at helping him.

One Possible Set of Answers

There are many good ways to answer these questions. In chapter one I briefly answered them to provide an approach that may differ from your own. Refer to those answers. Let me emphasize that the following answers are not "correct" but may be more or less helpful for Jim than yours. This different perspective demonstrates once again that helping does not mean finding the one "true" problem as much as it means finding a good way to help people change by using one of many true ways of thinking about problems.

(a) *What else would you like to know about Jim, especially what would you ask him the next time you talk?*

In addition to the six questions on page 22, I would want to ask more about his behavior. For example, I would ask:

7. Have you done anything to merit the label of "Jesus freak"?

8. How close is your relationship with your girlfriend?

9. How, specifically, do you act when you get "bitter" and "angry"? What particular situations result in this behavior?

(b) *What do you think Jim's biggest problem(s) is (are)?*

First, I would want to know what *Jim* thinks his biggest problems are. I suspect that Jim is most concerned about either the troublesome parts of his Christian life or his depression. He probably considers the two intimately related, but I would probe to determine whether he sees any connection and, if so, to what extent. Jim's answers to these questions would determine my actions.

(c) *How would you like Jim to think about his problems?*

At least two convenient ways are available to link all of Jim's problems. One way is to view them as products of a disrupted spiritual life. The sins are due to his deficient relationship with God, and the negative emotions (anxiety and depression) are the natural consequences. The other way to link Jim's problems is to view them as indications of a general loss of control. He feels unable to control the reactions of his friends, the views of his girlfriend, the appearance of various sins, his recurring nervousness, his "whirling mind" which prevents sufficient sleep and his depression. Jim's feeling that he might "lose it" could mean that he recognizes his impending loss of control.

Let me emphasize that these are only two of many ways to think about Jim's problems. They are not necessarily the only or the correct ways. Jim undoubtedly has a disrupted relationship with God. He feels that he might lose control. Both of these conceptualizations emphasize part of the truth about Jim's problems. As humans, we cannot understand the whole truth; as helpers, we should not try. We must concentrate on the part of the truth that allows Jim to make productive changes in his life. Therefore, I would choose one of these two ways and try to help Jim rethink his emotional problems accordingly. I would probably choose a way that Jim did *not* suggest because I know that he must change to solve his emotional problems.

(d) *What goals do you have?*

My goals would be determined by the way in which Jim came to rethink the cause of his problems. If he reconceptualized his problem as the result of a disrupted relationship with God, the goal is obvious—restore a right relationship with God. If loss of control was his verdict, the goal is to restore control to his life.

(e) *What would you try to get Jim to do about his problems?*

Disrupted relationship with God: we would plan ways to get Jim closer to God. This might include his joining a Christian group. It might involve reading Christian books about his problems or listening to recordings of Christian speakers. I would encourage him to pray specifically about problem areas and to combat his sinful behavior by praying for strength. Jim could study God's assurances in the Bible about his control and about Jesus' admonitions to cast our anxiety on him.

Loss of control: Jim could endeavor with the Lord's help to restore control to various areas of his life. I would encourage him to study God's promises that he will protect and defend us, and that he has things well in hand. With this foundational belief Jim could systematically attack each problem area. Fellowship with Christians could counteract his lack of support from other friends and from his girlfriend. By prayer and self-control he can practice and "take every thought captive to obey Christ" (2 Cor 10:5) to control his anger, bitterness and bad language. To control his gossip, he can practice controlling his tongue by giving it to God and substituting blessing for cursing (Jas 3:8, 10). To control his anxiety, Jim can ponder the trustworthiness of God and behave as if he were not anxious.

Both conceptualizations lead to similar (but not identical) action plans. The reasons the helper gives for each strategy are different. Inducing a person to take action to change a situation usually requires persuasion.

(f) *How might you accomplish this?*

I would help Jim see that each of his problems is related to the new way of conceptualizing the cause. Then I would find out exactly what things Jim would like to be different in the case of each problem. He would specify his goals as precisely as possible. Finally, we would systematically examine each problem. Throughout the helping relationship we would talk about the events in his life and how they related to the new conceptualization of the problem and to his goals.

(g) *How would you know if you were successful?*

If Jim reached the goals he had set for himself, we succeeded. If not, we failed. My feelings about the attempt—be they pride or shame, relief or frustration—are not the measure of my partnership with Jim.

What Have You Learned?

A vital lesson of this book is to recognize your limitations as a helper. Unless you already have extensive supervised experience at counseling others, you should not attempt to counsel people who are seriously disturbed. There is no sin in admitting this. Becoming competent to counsel people who are seriously disturbed requires systematic knowledge of psychological disorders, a clear idea about how to help, previous practice at counseling while being supervised by a trained professional and thoughtful evaluation of your attempts to help. Learn to determine when you can be directly helpful and when you should refer a person to someone else.

On the other hand, you should be able to help more effectively those God has called you to help. I hope this book has helped you become even more proficient at doing those things that friends do well, including understanding, offering an objective viewpoint, giving timely advice, and providing loyal support and follow-up. Remember that effective helping involves numerous skills, and like any other complex behavior will improve with experience. Grow, stretch and improve, recognizing that your performance will vary from day to day and from friend to friend.

I have been a helper, too, trying to help you become a more effective helper. My efforts have followed the model for helping proposed in this book. First, I talked to many people, both within and outside the church, to understand their concerns about aiding friends. Second, I have continually tried to help you rethink how you help others by developing this simple, five-step model. Third, by means of specific instructions and case studies, I have worked with you to develop action plans for helping people with emotional problems.

Yet despite my efforts, the real learning takes place when you put these ideas and plans into practice. As in any helping relationship, reading books and talking about strategies have their limitations. To use the gift of helping effectively you must step out in faith, relying wholly on God. When you try my suggestions some may not work for you; some will. Some of my suggested action plans will not fit your style; some will. Many of the suggestions will not fit your friends because I have concentrated on a general model for any helper and not on how to help people rethink specific problems. You will develop your style and find your own effective action plans to help others solve the specific problems they encounter.

My formal relationship with you is ending, so the support that I provide will be through prayer. Any follow-up must come only as you write to me about the things that did and did not work. My hopes and prayers are with you as you begin this adventure of helping.

Notes

Chapter 1

[1]"Differential Functioning of Lay and Professional Helpers," *Journal of Counseling Psychology* 15 (1968):117.

[2]W. F. Brown, "Effectiveness of Paraprofessionals: The Evidence," *Personnel and Guidance Journal* 53 (1974): 257-63; A. Hoffman and R. Warmer, "Paraprofessional Effectiveness," *Personnel and Guidance Journal* 54 (1976): 494-97.

[3]Gary Collins, *How to Be a People Helper* (Santa Ana, Calif.: Vision House, 1976).

[4]Lawrence Crabb, *Effective Biblical Counseling* (Grand Rapids, Mich.: Zondervan, 1977).

[5]Paul Welter, *How to Help a Friend* (Wheaton, Ill.: Tyndale, 1978).

Chapter 2

[1]C. S. Lewis, *Mere Christianity* (New York: Macmillan, 1946); Francis Schaeffer, *The God Who Is There* (Downers Grove, Ill.: InterVarsity

Press, 1968); id., *He Is There and He Is Not Silent* (Wheaton, Ill.: Tyndale, 1972); id., *The Church before the Watching World* (Downers Grove, Ill.: InterVarsity Press, 1971).

²J. B. Phillips, *Your God Is Too Small* (New York: Macmillan, 1964), pp. 75-88.

³Lewis, p. 6.

⁴Gary Collins, ed., *Helping People Grow: Practical Approaches to Christian Counseling* (Santa Ana, Calif.: Vision House, 1980). This book summarizes several approaches to Christian counseling.

Chapter 3

¹Victor Frankl, *Man's Search for Meaning* (New York: Pocket Books, 1963).

²Erich Fromm, *The Sane Society* (Greenwich, Conn.: Fawcett Publications, 1955), pp. 64-66.

³For example, *The God Who Is There* and *Escape from Reason* (Downers Grove, Ill.: InterVarsity Press, 1968).

⁴C. S. Lewis, *The Last Battle* (New York: Macmillan, 1956); id., *The Great Divorce,* (New York: Macmillan, 1946).

⁵Jay Adams, *Competent to Counsel* (Nutley, N.J.: Presbyterian and Reformed Publishing Co., 1970); id., *The Christian Counselor's Manual* (Grand Rapids, Mich.: Baker Book House, 1973).

⁶Albert Ellis and Robert A. Harper, *A New Guide to Rational Living* (Englewood Cliffs, N.J.: Prentice-Hall, 1975).

⁷Aaron Beck, *Cognitive Therapy and the Emotional Disorders* (New York: International Universities Press, 1976).

⁸Victor Raimy, *Misunderstandings of the Self* (San Francisco: Jossey-Bass, 1975).

⁹Eric Berne, *Games People Play* (New York: Grove Press, 1964); Thomas Harris, *I'm OK—You're OK: A Practical Guide to Transactional Analysis* (New York: Harper & Row, 1969); Claude Steiner, *Scripts People Live: Transactional Analysis of Life Scripts* (New York: Bantam, 1975); id., *Games Alcoholics Play* (New York: Ballantine, 1977).

¹⁰Carl Rogers, *Client-Centered Therapy* (Boston: Houghton Mifflin, 1965).

¹¹Sigmund Freud, *Introductory Lectures on Psychoanalysis,* trans. James Strachey (New York: W. W. Norton & Co., 1966; originally published 1917).

¹²Albert Bandura, *Principles of Behavior Modification* (New York: Holt, Rinehart & Winston, 1969); Joseph Wolpe, *Psychotherapy by Reciprocal Inhibition* (Stanford: Stanford University Press, 1958); Carl E. Thoresen and Michael J. Mahoney, *Behavioral Self-Control* (New York: Holt, Rinehart & Winston, 1974).

[13]Jay Haley, *Problem Solving Therapy* (San Francisco: Jossey-Bass, 1978).

Chapter 4
[1]Erich Fromm, *The Art of Loving* (New York: Bantam Books, 1956).
[2]Erich Fromm, *The Sane Society.*
[3]Thomas Kuhn, *The Structure of Scientific Revolutions* (Chicago: University of Chicago Press, 1970).
[4]Thomas Kuhn, *The Essential Tension: Selected Studies in Scientific Tradition and Change* (Chicago: University of Chicago Press, 1977), pp. ix-xxiii.

Chapter 5
[1]Virginia Satir, *Conjoint Family Therapy* (Palo Alto: Science and Behavior Books, 1967).
[2]Albert Mehrabian, *Tactics of Social Influence* (Englewood Cliffs, N.J.: Prentice-Hall, 1970).
[3]H. H. Strupp, S. W. Hadley and B. Gomez-Schwartz, *Psychotherapy for Better or Worse* (New York: Jason Aronson, 1977).
[4]Richard Bandler and John Grinder, *The Structure of Magic,* vol. I (Palo Alto: Science and Behavior Books, 1975).
[5]Joan S. Zaro et al., *A Guide for Beginning Psychotherapists* (Cambridge: Cambridge University Press, 1977).
[6]Jay Haley, *Strategies of Psychotherapy* (New York: Grune & Stratton, 1963).

Chapter 6
[1]Sigmund Freud, *The Interpretation of Dreams,* trans. James Strachey (New York: Avon, 1965; originally published 1899); Carl Rogers, *Client-Centered Therapy.*
[2]Freud, *Introductory Lectures.*
[3]Rogers, *Client-Centered Therapy.*
[4]B. F. Skinner, *Beyond Freedom and Dignity* (New York: Alfred A. Knopf, 1971).
[5]William Hinds, "Emotions in Psychotherapy" (paper presented in a workshop at the University of Missouri-Columbia Counseling Services, 1977).

Chapter 7
[1]Freud, *The Interpretation of Dreams* and *Introductory Lectures.*
[2]Freud, *Introductory Lectures.*
[3]Sigmund Freud, " 'Wild' Psychoanalysis," *Standard Edition* (London: Hogarth Press, 1957), 11:221-27.

Chapter 8

[1]C. S. Lewis, *Miracles* (New York: Macmillan, 1947), p. 141.

[2]Zaro et al., p. 41.

[3]Haley, *Problem Solving Therapy*, pp. 20-21.

[4]Arnold Lazarus, *Behavior Therapy and Beyond* (New York: McGraw-Hill, 1971), pp. 81-82.

[5]Strupp, Hadley and Gomez-Schwartz.

[6]R. Bruce Sloane et al., *Psychotherapy versus Behavior Therapy* (Cambridge: Harvard University Press, 1975), p. 21.

[7]A. Mehrabian and H. Reed, "Factors Influencing Judgments of Psychopathology," *Psychological Reports* 24 (1969): 323-30.

[8]Allen E. Bergin, "Psychotherapy and Religious Values," *Journal of Consulting and Clinical Psychology* 48 (1980): 95-105.

[9]Zaro et al., p. 116.

[10]Ibid., pp. 117-18.

[11]Haley, *Problem Solving Therapy*, pp. 33ff.

[12]Zaro et al., pp. 118-21.

Chapter 9

[1]See, for example, Matthew 6:8; 7:7; 21:22; Luke 11:9-13; John 14:13; 15:7; 16:24; James 1:5; 4:2; 1 John 3:22; 5:14.

[2]Carl Rogers, "The Necessary and Sufficient Conditions of Therapeutic Personality Change," *Journal of Consulting Psychology* 21 (1957): 95-103.

[3]Robert R. Carkhuff, *Helping and Human Relations* (New York: Holt, Rinehart & Winston, 1969); Gerald Egan, *The Skilled Helper: A Model for Systematic Helping and Interpersonal Relating* (Monterey, Calif.: Brooks/Cole, 1975); Allen E. Ivey and Norma B. Gluckstern, *Basic Attending Skills: Participant Manual* (Amherst, Mass.: Microtraining Associates, 1974); id., *Basic Influencing Skills: Participant Manual* (Amherst, Mass.: Microtraining Associates, 1976); David R. Evans et al.) *Essential Interviewing: A Programmed Approach to Effective Communication* (Monterey, Calif.: Brooks/Cole, 1979).

[4]Ivey and Gluckstern, *Influencing Skills*, pp. 53-57.

[5]Robert R. Carkhuff et al., *The Skills of Helping: An Introduction to Counseling Skills* (Amherst, Mass.: Human Resource Development Press, 1979).

[6]Egan, pp. 137-41.

Chapter 10

[1]Bandler and Grinder, pp. 39-54.

[2]Everett L. Shostrum, producer, *Three Approaches to Psychotherapy* (Santa Ana, Calif.: Psychological Films, 1966).

[3]Os Guinness, *The Dust of Death* (Downers Grove, Ill.: InterVarsity Press, 1973), p. 360.

Chapter 11
[1]Welter, esp. pp. 186-263.
[2]Haley, *Problem Solving Therapy,* p. 53.
[3]K. Daniel O'Leary, "The Effects of Self-Instruction on Immoral Behavior," *Journal of Experimental Child Psychology* 6 (1968): 297-301.
[4]John Monahan and K. Daniel O'Leary, "Effects of Self-Instruction on Rule-Breaking Behavior," *Psychological Reports* 29 (1972): 1059-66.
[5]Richard N. Bolles, *What Color Is Your Parachute? A Practical Manual for Job Hunters and Career Changers,* 5th ed. rev. (Berkeley, Calif.: Ten Speed Press, 1979).

Chapter 13
[1]Carkhuff.